THE PRINCE OF TRICKS

Luther Tsai has achievements worldwide as an architect, urban planner, author and academic. From creating spaces in the most vibrant cities of modern Asia to creating innovative Humanities, Science, English and Mandarin curriculum worldwide, Luther and his wife, Serene Pang, the education consultant for this series, recreate the remarkable vision of ancient China found in the Magic Mirror series.

Nury Vittachi is an author based in Hong Kong. His writing is 'endearingly wacky', said *The Times* of London and 'heading for cult status' according to the *Herald-Sun* of Australia. Vittachi has had regular broadcasting slots on the BBC and CNN. 'Dr Who' star David Tennant recently recorded an audiobook version of a Vittachi tale.

For instructions to make the Sun of Majapahit, go to page 146.

The sunburst symbol is found in many ruins of the era and thought to be the emblem of the Majapahit Empire.

Magic Mirror

Mysteries...

The Prince of Tricks

LUTHER TSAI & NURY VITTACHI

SCHOLASTIC
New York Toronto London Auckland
Sydney New Delhi Hong Kong

Dedicated to my father who left to me the gift of dreaming, and my wife Serene who helps make my dreams come true. With love to my two children T & T.
Luther Tsai

To the children of Asia who live in a region with a rich but under-celebrated history.
Nury Vittachi

Published by Scholastic India Pvt. Ltd.
A subsidiary of Scholastic Inc., New York, 10012 (USA).
Publishers since 1920, with international operations in Canada, Australia, New Zealand, the United Kingdom, India, and Hong Kong.

For information regarding permission, write to:
Scholastic India Pvt. Ltd.
A-27, Ground Floor, Sigma Centre
Infocity-1, Sector 34, Gurgaon 122001 (India)

First edition: December 2016
This reprint edition: May 2025

ISBN-13: 978-93-86313-61-4

Printed at Shivam offset Press, New Delhi

What is Real?

'Now we see but a poor
Reflection as in a mirror ...
Now I know in part ...
Then I shall know fully, even
As I am fully known.'

In this story, facts and whispers of real life people are here for you to find.
The rest of the story is made up of shadows and reflections, fleeting images of people and events that remain, and haunt us still.

Look inside the Magic Mirror.

1

The Forest Princeling

In a small house in the heart of a dense white orchid forest lived a poor widow with four girls.

The family name was Kleting and the mother gave the children colours as names:

Abang, meaning "Red", was the oldest.

Biru, meaning "Blue", came second.

Ijo, meaning "Green", was the third.

And Kuning, meaning "Yellow", was the youngest.

The girls were full of life and laughter, and the parents hoped for good marriages for them.

'You need to be beautiful and act in a refined way to have a good future,' said the mother. 'So practise the right skills.'

But little Yellow, Kleting Kuning, was not like the others. She loved nature and would spend hours wandering through the forest.

Her mother was often frustrated with her. 'Kleting Kuning,' she would say, 'why can't you spend your time sewing clothes and making yourself beautiful like your sisters?'

'I like to explore,' Kuning replied.

One day, Kleting Kuning was in the depths of the woods when she heard someone approaching. She quickly shimmied up a tree.

She saw a nervous boy, who seemed to be lost. He had come from the direction of a town near the western edge of the forest.

He did not look dangerous, and seemed to be about her age.

So she jumped out of the tree, appearing in front of him like an angel dropped from heaven.

'Are you lost?' she asked.

'No,' he lied, trying to sound brave. 'Not at all! I'm a great prince, exploring the royal forests, and I know exactly where I am. The city is that way,' he cried, pointing in the wrong direction.

Kuning laughed at his answer, and he laughed too. She could see that he had a tendency to make things up, but she didn't mind.

'Great prince, I will show you around,' said Kleting Kuning. She made him feel less worried by showing him the places where she liked to play, and later, she showed him the path out of the forest, to the town.

They started to meet regularly, and they developed nicknames for each other. She was the Sky Angel, and he was the Lost Prince.

After many weeks, the Lost Prince said to the Sky Angel that he wouldn't be back for a while.

'My father, the great king, says a great prince needs to go to a great school. So he is sending me far away to be educated.'

'Right,' said the Sky Angel. 'I'll wait for you.'

But the Lost Prince never returned.

Kleting Kuning often visited the spot where they used to play, but he was never there.

Then, after a year, Kuning left a little hidden sign there, which she knew only he would be able to see: a note in a hole in the tree where he had first met the Sky Angel.

She returned a week later, to find it untouched. She didn't go back.

Years passed, and the Kleting family was ready to find husbands for their girls.

There were not many choices in that part of the world, so there was much rejoicing when news arrived that a young man had returned to the region and his parents were looking for a bride.

Could he be Kleting Kuning's lost prince?

She listened to the adults talk, but was sad to hear that he was neither a village boy nor a great prince, but the son of a prosperous merchant. The young man was called Ande Ande Lumut, and he came from a great manor house far from the forest, across the wide river.

His father had organised a party so he could meet the young people of the area.

Kleting Mama decided that she wanted him to marry one of her girls—but not Kleting Kuning. It would be wrong if he liked her, since she was young and foolish and did nothing to beautify herself.

She gave all the girls fine clothes to wear, except for little Yellow, whom she put into an old dress.

Then she gave them all gifts to carry, but not Kleting Kuning. The old woman saw a broom that someone had dropped on the road outside her house, and she gave that to her.

'But I will look like a servant if I carry the broom,' the girl said.

'A broom is a lucky gift,' said the mother, although it wasn't true at all.

She told the girls that they must each arrive separately, so that Ande Ande Lumut could spend time with each of them and make his choice. 'And Kuning must go last,' she said. 'Because she is the youngest.'

In truth, Kleting Kuning did not mind. In her heart, she was still waiting for the return of her friend.

When the first daughter, Kleting Abang, reached the riverside, she realised there was a problem.

The boat service across the water was run by a crab-catcher who stank of seafood. And he said: 'The payment for crossing is a kiss.'

The girl thought this was a bad situation, but she could not think of anything else to do, so she gave him the kiss he had demanded.

And he took her over the water.

The second daughter, Kleting Biru faced the same problem—and she also gave a kiss to the crab-man.

And so it was for the third daughter, Kleting Ijo.

Kleting Kuning was allowed to leave her home last, and hurried as she went, knowing that the party would be almost over by the time she reached it.

When she got to the river, the crab man demanded a kiss.

'Certainly not!' she said, and marched away.

But then what could she do?

How could she cross the river without a boat? The sun was setting, and the party would nearly be over.

She went to the shallowest part of the river, but still could find no way across.

Then she swept at the water with her broom and noticed a stepping stone just under the surface.

She jumped onto it. She swept at the water again, and found another stepping stone, just out of sight.

She jumped onto that one too.

And so she made it all the way across the river.

When she arrived at the party, she could see her sisters sitting unhappily together on one side of the garden.

It seemed that the young businessman, Ande Ande Lumut, hated the smell of seafood more than anything else in the world.

And the three girls smelled of the crab-man.

Ande Ande Lumut had rejected them all.

But there was something else. He was telling his parents that he did not want to marry *any* girl they found for him.

He had given his heart to a girl he had met many years ago, and she was the one he wanted to find, he explained. This sort of party was useless.

He stepped away from his parents, in a sad mood, and mounted a horse, to ride into the forest.

As he set off, he heard a voice calling him from the trees.

'Ande Ande Lumut,' said the voice.

He rode into the woods.

But there was nobody there.

He thought he heard someone whisper his name from the trees on one side. He approached them.

Kleting Kuning jumped from a tree and landed in front of him.

'Sky Angel,' he said.

'Lost Prince,' she replied.

2

A Call to Adventure

'What a cute story,' Miranda Lee said out loud, lowering the book. 'It's like one of those classic fairy tales that they make into Barbie movies or Disney tales. Funny it's not *that* famous.'

She decided that her parents had been cruel to her by not naming her after a colour. Colours as names were cool. Perhaps she could give herself one? But what colour should she have?

Yellow was a nice colour, but not a particularly attractive name.

Red? That was better: kind of cool. Miranda Red Lee. It had a ring to it.

Other colours were probably not so good. Green and Brown sounded like the family names of British accountants. Black sounded like a character in a game—wasn't there a Dr Black in that board game where you had to find the murderer?

Then it occurred to her that there were some even more interesting colours available if you went past the basic colours of the rainbow—her favourite colour was purple, which would not make a nice name, but maybe magenta, which was sort of purplish, would work. Or lilac. Or maroon.

Hmm. Which would it be? Magenta ... that was the nicest.

But then she had another thought. Turquoise? Did Turquoise Lee work as a name? No, everyone would call her Turk or Turkey, which would not be good.

She decided to tell her brother that from now on, she was to be addressed as Magenta, short for Miranda Magenta Lee.

She would have a word with her parents, when they got back from their travels, to make it official.

If they ever got back from their travels.

She'd stopped caring—or so she told herself. Deep down, she knew she felt angry and neglected.

'Strange that this story is not more famous,' she repeated.

She was talking to her brother Marko, although he didn't respond, being lost in his own book. He gave a slight grunt to acknowledge that she had spoken, but she knew he hadn't really heard her.

***

The two siblings were sitting in big leather armchairs in their grandfather's study.

The old man had, as usual, given them an assignment. Also, as usual, their task had arrived in the shape of a parcel and a letter with some instructions. Like their parents, their grandfather too was constantly on the road.

Now you might think that most children who were told to study something by adults who were not even present might find excuses to avoid doing as they were told. And indeed, Miranda Lee often did search for good reasons to be 'too busy' to do any studying.

But she knew that her grandfather's instructions were worth following as they always led to an adventure. And this one was sure to be a very exciting one too.

She had been given a difficult homework assignment: she had to write a history essay on a subject of her choice, and it had to be something that would be new and fresh to the rest of the class. That meant that they couldn't just take something out of the school history textbooks.

She didn't know where to begin. The assignment had been set by the school's new history teacher, Mr Tork, and she wanted to make a good impression on him.

That was the question she had been wrestling with, when, by good luck or design, the job that grandfather had lined up for them arrived, and it seemed that it might just fit the bill.

She could tell it was going to be an intriguing task as soon as she opened the package, which had arrived earlier that day.

It contained four things. One was some sort of small disk made of stone, a bit like a big, thick coin. It looked very old, and had the design of the sun on one side, and some odd lines on the other, like a pattern made of squares and rectangles. The next was a letter addressed to the two children. And there were two books as well.

The letter had a title on it, which may be unusual for most people (as, indeed, the writing of letters themselves had become unusual even during those days), but it was pretty normal for Grandpa.

"Interesting Forgotten Kingdoms of South-east Asia 1", it said. "Majapahit: Land of Trickster Princes".

Miranda Lee had never heard of the place, but she liked the sound of "Interesting Forgotten Kingdoms", so she was happy to think that she would investigate something interesting.

And honestly, although she hated to be thought of as what is sometimes called a "girly girl" (she considered herself a feminist), she liked the idea of a land of princes, whether they were tricksters or otherwise.

Would there be pictures of handsome princes in the books that accompanied the letter? She wouldn't mind finding her own Ande Ande Lumut.

She lowered the letter and looked at the books grandfather had sent.

One of the volumes was a factual one: *The Culture and History of Majapahit*.

Miranda picked it up and flicked through it. It looked a bit dry. On the plus side, it had a lot of photographs in it, many in colour.

But no handsome princes.

She turned to the other book, which was very different. It was called *Tales from the Lost Kingdom of Majapahit*. It was a book of stories. So, she quickly grabbed that book and began reading it.

'This one is for me,' she said to her brother who was looking at the little disk that was in the package. 'The other one is for you.'

'How do you know?' Marko asked suspiciously. 'Does Grandpa say that in the letter?' He was turning the coin-like thing over and over in his hands, trying to decipher the strange pattern on one side.

'No, but it's obvious,' Mira said. 'This one has stories, the sort of stories which are more suitable for someone like me, who likes love stories and stuff, while the other has facts, which are for nerdy bookish people like you.'

Marko looked at his sister with a resigned expression, but said nothing.

Miranda kept her eyes on the storybook. She knew that he knew she had chosen the book that *looked* more interesting. And there was nothing Marko could do about it.

Mira settled into a comfortable position in the armchair and started reading.

Her brother picked up the other book and flicked it open.

***

Although few people know much about it today, Majapahit had been a great empire in the past, Marko Lee's book said.

It grew out of a smaller kingdom in the 1200s, called the Singhasari.

By the mid-1300s, Majapahit was extremely rich.

One reason it grew so fast over the centuries was that it had cunning and resourceful leaders, and the other was its position, as a key stop on the spice trade route—the path that international traders took to collect delectable Asian spices they could sell in the West.

Marko realised that the "cunning and resourceful leaders" might be the "trickster princes" that grandfather's letter had mentioned.

'South-east Asia supplied the whole world with spices and seasonings, which transformed cookery around the world,' the book said. 'What would desserts be without sugar and cinnamon? What would curries be without coriander and cumin and turmeric and fenugreek?'

He flicked to another page.

'The empire of Majapahit grew physically large and swallowed up many places which today are separate countries, provinces or states,' said a caption below a map of South-east Asia.

He read on: 'The string of landmasses which we know today as the Malay Archipelago, including Indonesia and Malaysia, were almost all part of Majapahit. The leaders then advanced on the kingdom of Singapura, and took that too.'

Singapura, Marko thought, must surely be modern-day Singapore.

'Today, to find land that belonged at one time to Majapahit, you only have to visit Indonesia, Malaysia, Singapore, Brunei, Thailand, East Timor and the southern parts of the Philippines and Thailand,' the book said.

The boy was surprised.

All those modern places were all part of a single, huge, lost and forgotten kingdom! Who would have imagined?

He returned to the preliminary pages of the book so that he could scan the contents page and see what else was in it.

One of the great things about factual books, as opposed to fiction, was that you didn't necessarily have to read everything in the order presented. You could go straight to whatever you thought were the most interesting bits.

He browsed the chapter headings.

Then he flicked through the pages until he came to a section called "Clues to the lost empire you can still see today".

It started by focussing on architecture. He was fascinated to see a picture of what he thought was a Bali-style gate. These were very unusual. Each gate post was a tall and highly ornate tower on three sides, and completely flat and featureless on the fourth—the side of the gate that faced its partner. It was as if a single structure had been made, and then split into two with a huge knife. It made the gate look like some sort of magic portal—especially since the gates were often not a part of walls, but just stood there by themselves.

Marko read on to discover that archaeologists acquired details of the lost kingdom when they had dug up ruins of a great ancient capital.

If you go to the island of Java, in Indonesia, you can see the ruins of an ancient capital in the city now known as Trowulan, the book said.

'It was lost for many years, but modern technology, such as satellite imaging systems, showed that the old capital of Majapahit was still there, and was much larger than historians had originally believed.'

Marko then turned to the chapter named "Sources of Information". This told him that there were two important manuscripts. One was called the *Pararaton*, also known as the "Book of Kings", and was about 400 years old. The other was a poem and it was even older: the *Nagarakertagama* was written in a language called Old Javanese in 1365. It was written only about 70 years after the founding of Majapahit, so was considered relatively authentic.

The boy's eyes widened when he read that there were Chinese sources, too, including records of a visit by the great Chinese explorer Zheng He. This admiral was very important in Marko's life because of a previous adventure he had had. Zheng He (pronounced Jeng Her) had a translator named Ma Huan who was fascinated by Majapahit and wrote a detailed record of the kingdom a century after it was founded, covering culture and customs, and mentioning the land's leader.

That writer called the ruler "the King of Chao-wa". At first, modern investigators didn't know who this was or where he lived. But if you say it out loud, you realise that it is "the King of Java".

'This book is really interesting too,' Marko said to his sister. 'There used to be this really amazing and huge kingdom. It disappeared, but there are parts of it remaining today, if you know where to look.'

***

Mira had just finished reading the second short story in her book of tales. It was called "The Thief King of the Spiral River".

'It sounds like it was a bit of a fairy tale land,' she said. 'Full of forests and princes and people having adventures. I wouldn't mind a visit.'

Her brother smiled. He knew what was coming.

She turned and put her book down, picking up her grandfather's letter again. Her eyes scanned the text until she got to the end. She read the last paragraph out loud.

'The sun symbol was hidden away in the war. Please return it to the noble trickster prince tonight. But be careful. There's a war going on!'

Mira looked at her brother. 'We have to take this coin thing to someone. Here, you carry it.'

She picked the small stone disc up from the table and handed it to him.

'I don't think it's a coin,' he said.

'Sure it is,' she said. 'Look at the size of it. It's exactly right for a coin. I'll show you.'

She reached over to her grandfather's desk and picked up a rather ornate old piggy bank he had.

Then she dropped the disk into the slot on the top. It just about fit through the hole, slightly scraping the sides.

'Perfect fit,' she said. 'See? It probably is some sort of coin.'

He frowned. 'Why did you do that? We need to take it with us if we're going on a trip.'

'We can get it out. There's always a plastic plug thing underneath a piggy bank where you can open it. Don't you know that?'

She turned the piggy bank over ... and ... a frown clouded

her face. There was no opening hatch. 'Where's the plug thing?' she asked.

He looked over at it. 'There's no opening. That's some sort of antique piggy bank. You'll have to shake it out—*if* you can.'

Mira looked worried. The disk had only just squeezed through the slot. Shaking it out was going to be hard—perhaps impossible.

'We'll have to break it.'

'No! We can't do that. It might be ancient and valuable.'

'Well, you get it out then.'

She handed the piggy bank to her brother and he peered into it.

He turned it around in his hands. 'There must be some way of opening it—perhaps there's a secret button that you press, and it opens.'

The boy started prodding and pressing at the bank.

Mira waited impatiently for a few seconds before snatching it out of his hands. 'Let me do it.'

But after a minute she realised that she couldn't find an opening either.

'Let's take it with us,' she said. 'Then we'll have time to open it while we look for whoever we have to deliver it to.'

This seemed the only solution. Marko put the piggy bank in the red school backpack he always carried.

Mira envisioned the trip ahead of them—she saw her brother doing the hard work, tracking down the address the little disk had to go to, while she spent her time talking to some handsome lost prince or stranger.

If this was the land of trickster princes, there had to be a few interesting guys around. And wasn't it true that cheeky guys were often more fun than polite ones? Like in *Pride and Prejudice*?

***

As night fell, Miranda and Marko Lee went over to an ornate box on their grandfather's old desk.

They took out a circular object from it, like a plate, but very old, and covered with carvings. It was made of a sort of metallic ore.

This was a classical Chinese item known as a "magic mirror". Usually it was polished on one side, so you could use it to look at yourself. And on the other side were intricate carvings. You can see magic mirrors in museums or on the internet, if you search for them.

They were known as magic mirrors because they really did seem to have strange powers. When you put them into places with a lot of light, it seemed as if light went through them, and projected images containing lines and shapes onto surfaces like walls and floors. The curious thing was that these images were often not the same as the images carved into the mirror. They seemed to come from inside the mirror somehow. Nobody quite knew how this was done. It was perhaps possible if you had hi-tech machinery and used laser beams to make micro-fine indentations invisible to the human eye. But magic mirrors were old, and came into existence long before such equipment was invented.

So they were mysterious and intriguing—and thus were called magic mirrors.

Mira and Marko used to hold up the mirror to the light shining through the window in the study. The light from the moon shone onto the magic mirror.

They stood under the mirror as the light shone through it, and the lines projected by the mirror formed an image on the floor and walls of the study. Now, here we have a choice about what to believe. The children insisted that the light used to get brighter and brighter, and then they would find themselves in the period of history they had been studying—as time travellers.

Mira and Marko's teacher friend Anya knew about their adventures, but she didn't believe in time travel. She thought that the children would spend hours reading books about a certain period, and then play games in which they imagined they went back to that time in history.

But it doesn't matter which version you prefer. The results were always the same.

***

As darkness fell, Mira and Marko held the mirror up to the moonlight coming through the circular window in their grandfather's study.

The moon seemed to shine its cold silver-blue light right through the magic mirror. And then, for Mira and Marko, the magic happened: the light started to grow in intensity. It became increasingly dazzling until it was white and bright, like the sun on a summer's day.

The two children shut their eyes tight. They heard a roaring sound and it seemed as if the light began to penetrate through their eyelids. The darkness in front of them turned pink-brown.

And then the glare faded.

Mira and Marko opened their eyes to find themselves no longer in grandfather's study, but somewhere quite different.

They were in a forest with many tropical plants and trees around them. White orchid trees stretched in all directions.

They could immediately tell that they were near the sea—there was the smell of salt in the air, and they could hear a distant rushing sound of waves crashing against the beach or rocks. It had been evening when they had left, but now they seemed to be in a slightly fading daylight, perhaps in the late afternoon. A sea breeze ruffled their hair.

But which way should they go?

They looked around them until they saw that they had materialised not far from a path.

'If we go that way, we'll head to the beach,' said Mira. 'Shall we try it?'

She was already setting off at high speed, and her brother had to move fast to catch up with her. She loved beach holidays.

'We're not here for sunbathing or relaxing on a beach,' said Marko. 'We have a job to do. I think we should go the other way—it must lead to the nearest town. We're more likely to find this noble trickster prince in a palace or something.'

'Not necessarily,' said his sister. 'Princes probably also like going to the beach, and they have more time to do that sort of thing, since they don't have normal jobs, right?'

She was walking steadily towards the water and he followed reluctantly.

'Slow down,' he complained.

Miranda did not slow down.

'You can go the other way if you like,' she said. 'I'll go this way. And then we can meet up later.'

But the path took them round a corner and what they saw caused both of them to come to a halt.

It led up a steep hill. They knew the sea was not far away, but it seemed to be over a high ridge. It was going to be a tough climb.

Mira pursed her lips and twisted her mouth to one side.

'Perhaps you're right,' she conceded. 'Let's go back on the path. It will probably lead to people, and we'll need people to help us, tell us where to go, et cetera.'

But now Marko was the one who wanted to keep heading forward. There was something about the slope ahead that was calling to him. High hills were useful when you weren't sure where you were. They gave you a view of the whole district.

'I think it will be a good idea to go up this slope. See how high it is? We'll be able to scope out the whole area from the top—find out where we are and which way we should go. See if there's a palace where a prince could live.'

Mira's brows furrowed into angry lines. 'I'm not going all the way up there just to have a nice view. *You* go up there. I'll walk into the town. And then we'll meet back where we started, near those white flower trees, and decide what to do.'

The boy thought for a moment. 'Okay,' he said. 'That sounds like a good plan.' He was light on his feet, and didn't mind scrambling up a hill. 'When and where shall we meet again?'

'How long will it take to get to the top of that hill and back again?'

'I don't know. Maybe 20 minutes each way, and five minutes for a rest and a look around from the top?'

'So that's 45 minutes all together. Well, it's harder for me to know how long I will need, because we don't know how far the town is from here.'

Marko was staring inland. 'Oh yes, we do,' he said. 'Look!' He pointed upwards at the treetops.

Mira followed the line of his gaze and saw a thin stream of smoke rising above the forest canopy.

'Maybe the forest is burning?'

'I don't think so. The line of smoke is very thin. It's probably a cooking fire.'

'That's what I was going to say.'

'How far do you think it is?'

'Hard to say. Maybe a ten-minute walk? Or fifteen?'

Mira was suddenly anxious to get going. It could be because she had the story of a Forest Prince in her mind and imagined bumping into him on the outskirts of the woods.

'Meet back where we started in an hour,' she said, heading into the interior.

'Fine,' said her brother, and started walking up the hill.

3

The Lost Prince

Just over 10 minutes later, Mira had reached a village. There were some men sitting around a cooking fire and there were the remains of a meal at the side of the road.

'Excuse me, I'm looking for Majapahit,' she said. 'It's around here, right?'

The gnarled old man in front of her said nothing, but peered at her without smiling and pointed up a slight upward incline with his bony finger.

'Thanks,' said Mira.

She thought him rather surly, but decided to remain polite. After all, she was the stranger here.

The girl marched up the little hill and surveyed the scene from the top of it. There was not much to see. The slope ran down on the other side to open grasslands. There were a few fields, perhaps rice paddies, on the left. On the right, there was mostly scrubland, and a few coconut trees. Directly ahead of her, the hill ran down to a patch of thick grass, with a single tall, thin tree in the middle of it.

But there were no signs of any sort of village or town.

'Great,' she mumbled to herself. 'Don't they believe in signposts round here? What about the tourist trade? How are we supposed to cope?'

She marched down the slope, hoping to meet someone who could advise her on what to do next.

There was a little hut tucked behind some trees on one side, and she knocked at the door there. After half a minute, the door creaked open and a woman's face looked out.

'Majapahit?' Mira asked. 'Do you know where it is?'

The woman, who was middle-aged but already had streaks of grey hair, looked puzzled.

'I'm looking for Majapahit,' the girl repeated.

The woman pointed straight down to the bottom of the hill at the patch of grass with one tree in it.

'It's that way?' Mira asked. 'Thanks.'

'That's it,' the woman said. 'That tree.'

Now it was the girl's turn to be puzzled. 'That tree is Majapahit?'

The woman nodded.

With a shrug, Miranda Lee walked towards the tree. She reached it in a few minutes and then stood in front of it, not knowing what to do next.

There were no buildings in sight. There was nothing but

a field of low shrubs and a few primitive paths through a woodland, and this one lonely tree.

She spoke aloud, just for the comfort of hearing her own voice. 'I don't get it. Majapahit is not a place but a tree? What is going on?'

'Those were my thoughts exactly, a few months ago,' said the tree.

Mira took a step back. 'Who's there?'

There was movement behind the trunk of the tree, and a man stepped out from behind it. He had been sitting at its trunk, staring out into the grassy field, hidden from view.

'Majapahit is just a tree. There had been a time I was expecting so much more, just like you, young woman.'

He had thick shaggy dark hair and a heavy black moustache, but somehow he didn't scare her. His eyes were tired, rather than angry or crazy. And his clothes were very fine—he had a brownish-purple silk jerkin on, canvas-like baggy trousers, and a cloak of some thicker material, which had a velvety sheen.

A lost prince? Perhaps. Unfortunately he was too old for her—probably in his late twenties or early thirties. Maybe he had a younger brother? Or a son?

'Sorry to disturb you,' she said. 'I was looking for Majapahit and the Spiral River and the forest and stuff ... where princes may be hanging out.'

He made a quick movement with his head and focussed on her. Something she had said had caught his attention.

He took one step towards her.

She was a little nervous now, but resisted the temptation to step backwards.

'Did you say "Spiral River"?'

She nodded. 'Yes. Is it round here?'

'So I take it you are the messenger sent to me?' he asked.

'Ye...es,' she said, before she could stop herself. 'Erm ... I am the messenger.'

She had just noticed that he carried a short, curved sword in his belt. He might be dangerous. Best to have a legitimate reason for being here and having disturbed him.

But was "yes" the best answer? What did it commit her to?

'At least I might be,' she added, deciding to be a bit cagey. 'It depends on what kind of messenger you mean.'

'You don't look like an angel or a djinn.'

'Er ... we come in a variety of styles and, er ... sizes,' she said, realising that she sounded like a TV advertisement.

'What do you know about the Spiral River?'

She thought for a moment. What had been the exact name of the story she had just been reading? "The Thief King of the Spiral River"?

'Erm ... I know it's associated with a king,' she said. 'An er ... unusual type of king.' Best not to mention the word "thief", she decided, in case it insulted this guy, who looked like he might be part of a royal family. Could he be the "thief king" of the story? Or perhaps he was the king-to-be?

'So I'm assuming that you are the messenger I was told to expect,' he continued. 'And if so, what is your message?'

Mira's mind raced. What on earth should she say to this guy? How had she got so deep into this mess so quickly? She wished she had read that blasted story instead of just glancing at the title and putting it aside for later.

'The message is this,' she said. 'You must walk with me to the Spiral River.'

'Lead the way, then,' he said, gesturing with his palm.

'Sure thing,' said Mira.

She sent up a quick arrow prayer to the universe—'Help!'—and then started walking. There was only one path and two directions, so she had a fifty per cent chance of leading him in the right direction.

'It used to be this way,' she said, with fake confidence. 'Let's see if it's still there. It may have moved. It may be the other way now. We'll find out soon enough. If it's not there, we can try the other way.'

'The river may have moved?' he asked.

'Of course,' she said, trying to sound confident. 'They do that all the time around here. It's a ... umm ... natural geographic phenomenon.'

As they walked along the dirt track, she was surprised to see several other men, similar in age to the one whom Mira had met at the tree, but in humbler clothing, step out of another path to approach them. They were heavily armed, and had thick, rough garments.

'Your highness,' said the one leading the group of newcomers. 'You're moving? Do you wish to have company?'

The man she was walking with gave a sigh before replying. 'Thanks, Pakubuwana, but I think you can take the men to the encampment and let them stand down. I need to do a bit of study myself, and this young lady may be able to help me, if she is who I think she is. Heaven knows the men need a rest.'

Mira flashed a nervous smile at the men—who she realised were some sort of military body—but she felt increasingly worried.

"Highness", they had called him. He was a prince. But he had an army with him. And they looked tired and ragged, as if they were in the middle of a war. That's what Grandpa had said in the letter. What had she got herself into!

As they continued down the path, the man introduced himself as Raden Wijaya, and explained that he was the new ruler of a significant part of the land.

'The great forest of Trik has been granted to me by decree, by the new king,' he said. 'I'm lucky to have it, I suppose. I'm lucky to be alive, even.'

That was an odd thing to say, Mira thought. How should she reply? She should say something sympathetic.

'Er ... that's nice. Sounds like you had a pretty rough week. So who is the king now? I'm not really up to speed on local politics.'

He looked at her suspiciously.

She shrugged apologetically. 'Sorry.'

He spoke to her but with his eyes now focussed ahead.

'Perhaps you are too young to follow the affairs of the state, but if you live here, you are a subject of the state, so you need to know who rules you. As you must surely know, the kingdom changed hands recently. I was on the losing side. Most of the men of power on the losing side were put to death by the new ruler, a man named Jayakatwang. But I was fortunate. He decided that I was far enough removed from the main line of the previous royal family to be a threat. So he did not kill me, but gave me a piece of land to rule over. It was mentioned to me as the land of Majapahit, but when I got to that place, I found that that was merely the name of a type of tree, in the middle of a forest called Trik. It's about two days' travel in that direction.'

He waved his hands to encompass an area vaguely to their left.

Mira nodded. If she was going to continue her bluff and get out of this hole, she needed as much information as she could.

'The new king of the whole land has made you into something like a smaller king of a part of this place? So ... are you a prince, or like some sort of nobleman, or courtier, serving the new king?'

The moustached man turned his rather dark, hooded eyes to her. 'I am a prince and no lowly nobleman or courtier. And most importantly, I am certainly not serving the new king—quite the contrary.'

Her eyebrows rose. 'Are you going to, like, overthrow the king? The war has started, right?'

She suddenly started wishing that she had read the factual book that she had given her brother to read, instead of the book of stories that she had chosen. That book, surely, would have included the sort of historical details that she needed to know. Bother! And why wasn't her cursed brother here? He would know what to say to this guy ... what was his name? Raden something ... Wijaya ... that was it! Maybe she should have just led the prince to that hill that Marko was climbing, instead of hoping that this path led to the river mentioned in the book of stories about princes.

'By sundown, I will be about halfway through the process of regaining the kingdom,' the prince said. 'The insurrection has begun.'

On the plus side, she realised that she needed to know all this for her history homework—it was really useful. This would fill a page or two—assuming she got out of this alive.

'So, this is the exact week that you take over from, what was his name, Jayakatwang? Can you give me some details? I'll need dates and timelines and so on. A chart would be good.'

He narrowed his eyes as he looked at her. 'You ask a lot of questions for a messenger. Normally messengers deliver information, rather than gather it.'

Mira realised that she was being her typical self—rather bossy, as her friends called her, or assertive, as she liked to think of herself. Luckily, Raden—just Raden would do for now—didn't seem to mind too much. He gave her a sidelong glance, but there was more curiosity than hostility in it.

Mira decided that she should perhaps tone it down a little. Curtsey, perhaps? Keep her head bowed? Probably young women in this place were a bit more humble in front of a prince. On the other hand, if he thought she was an angelic messenger of some kind, then she might as well play up to his expectations. After all, you never hear of nervous angels, do you? Angels always started by saying "Fear not", so they were probably pretty calm and collected people, white nightdresses and halos notwithstanding.

'Excuse me, O Prince. What exactly is happening at sundown?' she asked. 'An insurrection has already started, you said?'

He glanced her way again and then looked into the distance before responding.

'We started fighting three days ago. I put my men into five troop formations. Four of them are attacking Tumapel now. If they make as good progress as I am hoping, they should have taken a third or perhaps half of the capital city by this time.'

Her mind raced. Where was Tumapel? She'd never heard of it. What should she say? 'And what about the fifth troop?' she asked.

'I brought the fifth troop here with me.'

'Why?'

'To see you.'

Mira's eyes widened. This was getting too weird. She had clearly been mistaken for someone. And she was getting herself into deeper and deeper trouble—trouble with a guy who carried a knife and who had an armed group of men with him.

'Are you absolutely sure that it's me you are looking for?'

'Yes,' Raden Wijaya said. 'You are a messenger called Mira, correct?'

Mira froze. She was speechless for a moment. How did he know her name?

'Yes,' she breathed, her heart hammering.

Clearly she was in the right place. But she had not the slightest idea what was going on.

***

After walking for another half an hour, Mira had the full story of the battle that had begun—and how the prince had ended up here, looking for her. Initially, all five of the prince's troop formations were poised to attack Tumapel, which was the capital city of the bad king—the guy's name was Jayakatwang and he was a vicious man who had killed many relatives of this prince.

Raden Wijaya's troops were far smaller in number than the king's defenders, and also less well-equipped. But he told her that they had a number of techniques up their sleeve. 'We use our wit and cunning where we cannot use force of numbers,' he said. 'We have surprises.'

Her mind raced. Maybe this was what Grandpa meant when he wrote about the "trickster princes".

'But I don't get it,' she had asked. 'Why are you here? Why did you leave the battle? And who told you my name?'

The prince's tone then changed, becoming more reflective. 'We'd just begun the battle of my life,' he said. 'I was fighting to become the king. I would have thought that nothing could have deflected me from it. Until I saw the light in the temple.'

'And that was your cue!' said Mira.

He turned to look at her.

'Um, sorry, that's just something we say in er ... the place I come from,' she stammered. 'So what was the light in the temple?'

'The temple was shining with a light quite different from the flames that would normally light a space like that at night—there was no flickering, no wavering, no swaying of shadows,' he said. 'It was a bright, slightly blue light—it was as if a piece of the day-time sky had fallen to the ground and been taken inside a house.'

The girl's mind raced. It sounded like an electric light. It was as if he had seen the light from a screen—maybe a television or a computer monitor or a smartphone. But how could that be?

'I went inside,' Wijaya continued, 'and followed the light around the corner into the central area of the building. There I saw a holy man. Some sort of wizard or djinn. The blue sunlight seemed to be coming from his hand.'

'What did he look like?' asked Mira, suddenly realising who he might be: her grandfather holding something, perhaps a smartphone. She pulled open the locket she kept around her neck and showed the picture of her grandfather to the prince.

'A tiny painting,' said the prince, 'and a perfect likeness. That's the man I saw.'

Mira was stumped. 'And he told you to come and see me? In the middle of the most important battle of your life? That doesn't make sense. And why would you obey?'

He nodded in agreement. 'True. It makes no sense. No leader would abandon his men in a battle like this. But it was what he said next that made me listen to him.'

'Go on.'

Raden Wijaya explained that the holy man had said that he knew the one thing that could stop him becoming the new king—whether he defeated the king of Tumapel or not.

There was a secret store of records—it was called the Ancient Knowledge—and it told the stories of his ancestors and gave details of his secret family tree. It also included a map of secret passages and doors in and around the palaces and the gardens of the royal family.

'There are almost no records of my family—think how unusual that is for a family of royal blood. It is said that my great grandfather committed some terrible deed and many of the family records were destroyed or hidden to cover up his wrongdoing. I have always known that the key to becoming king was not simply taking over Tumapel, but uncovering the hidden knowledge that awaits the man who would be the true king of this place. Jayakatwang knows nothing of the ancient knowledge, and neither does he care. The same could be said for the man he killed, Kertenegara.'

Raden Wijaya said the holy man had known this. 'The old man said to me that I was not really fighting to take over the palace, a mere building, but fighting to take my place in history, and I would need the ancient knowledge to do so. Your friend, the old man, is wise.'

'He's my grandfather.'

He looked at her face, as if he was trying to match her features to the man he had met.

'I don't look like him, which is hardly surprising, as I was adopted,' she said.

He raised his eyebrows to express curiosity. 'Divine messengers live in families, just like we do?' he asked.

She didn't know what to say.

But then he continued with his story. 'Your grandfather told me that I should let my men continue with the battle against the troops of the king. But that I myself should head to the coast, where I would meet a messenger underneath a majapahit tree. He said that your name would be Mira and you would lead me to the secret of my great-great-grandfather. He led me to believe that you would appear as an angel or a djinn or something of that nature.'

'That was enough to make you leave the battle?'

'Absolutely not. I had other very important reasons to come up to this part of the coast anyway—strategic ones—reasons I choose not to share with others. I had intended to send my deputy, Pakubuwana, but I trusted the old man, and agreed to do as he suggested. I left my other deputy in charge of the battle, and told him that I would return the following morning.'

'Right,' said Mira, trying to sound like this was all making sense to her.

Boy, was this complicated! It seemed as if her grandfather wanted the prince to get away from the battle to come up here to speak to her—but why? Perhaps it was that coin—maybe they had to deliver it to this guy?

'I do have something for you—a sort of coin-like thing. My ... er ... assistant is looking after it at the moment, but we can meet up with him soon,' the girl said.

'What I seek is information—knowledge about my great-great-grandfather—and a way to find out about the past. If I become king, I need to know the history of the kings of Singhasari.'

Mira nodded. 'I get that,' she said, although she had never heard of the place that he had just mentioned.

Maybe her grandfather had wanted her to read the story of the thief king and tell it to this guy. Maybe it was the story of his ancestor or something. But she had only read the title. What a shame they hadn't brought the book with them.

But perhaps there was a copy of the same book here? The story must have come from this part of the world, so it must be here somewhere. She looked at Raden Wijaya and saw that he seemed to be expecting information from her.

'Er ... let's start with you telling me what you know about your ancestors,' she said. 'To set the scene, sort of thing.'

Wijaya again looked into the distance as he spoke, pulling out information from deep memories.

'There are many strange legends about the founder of the Singhasari kingdom, but they don't add up at all. Some say he was a great man, the greatest of all men. Others say he was the worst of all men, a murderer and a robber and a thief. There is much about him that is hidden, and there is something in the legends that I need to know. But all the information about him has been destroyed, or hidden, or disguised as something else. The official historians' books and scrolls have blank pages where they should have facts.'

'And I am supposed to fill in the gaps?'

Wijaya nodded. 'Exactly. I waited under a majapahit tree and along you came, talking about the Spiral River.'

'I don't suppose one of your ancestors was a girl called Kleting Kuning?' she asked. 'Her name means "yellow". I can remember a fair bit about her.'

'No.'

'Or Ande Ande Lumut?'

'No.'

Mira decided that she desperately needed to change the subject. She clearly knew nothing at all about the man's ancestors.

'So what is it with this tree? What's so special about it? Maybe the fruit is special in some way? Maybe it is delicious and you are going to rule over an area which becomes rich and successful because of its fruit-farming. Like a thriving agricultural economy or something.'

He turned and flashed her a brief, ironic smile. 'That would have been nice, but *maja* means fruit, and *pahit* means bitter. The fruit of bitterness. The only special thing about this fruit is that you can't eat it. It's too sour and bitter, which is a bit like my temper at the moment. I feel close to my moment of triumph—and yet I am not ready.'

They walked in silence for a while. Mira's mind was racing. How could she give him information that she didn't have? Why had Grandpa put her in this situation?

They stepped through a clearing and found themselves approaching a small township. People sitting outside their huts rose to their feet and approached them.

'Where to now?' Raden Wijaya asked.

An idea flashed in Mira's mind. 'Stories,' she said. 'Find the village storyteller. Your answers will be there. You need to know about the thief king thief king of the Spiral River. It's a story, but it's based on something that really happened. I wonder if there's a book shop here? I wish you had e-books. E-books are so cool. You can just download them onto your phone, like instantly. But of course you don't even have phones. I mean, how do you people *live* without these things? We wouldn't be able to.'

The prince turned his head to look at her. He was not smiling. 'I understand so little of what you say. But you want me to talk to the village storyteller?' He sounded deeply sceptical.

'Yes,' said Mira. She felt like she was clutching at straws, but she couldn't think of anything else to do. 'Look—one thing I can do is to make a prophecy-type statement about the future. And I can guarantee that it's accurate. In the future, stories will be told around the world about the people of this region, and some will be about the king of the Spiral River. The storytellers here must already know the tales, otherwise how could the stories survive and find their way into books in the future? See?'

He gave her a quizzical look.

'You are a strange young woman.'

'I am a messenger, an angel, a djinn,' she said. 'I have seen the future. Honest! Truly. Ask me about anything in the future, like the internet or 3D movies or anything. You don't even know what they are, right? That proves it.'

She realised that to him it must seem like she was just babbling—but she was grateful when his next action suggested that he was going to give her a chance. He raised his voice and spoke to the approaching people. 'Do you have a village storyteller? I need some answers from the past.'

The villagers conferred with each other before replying.

'Sit and have tea,' an older man said. 'There is no storyteller here, but there is a very great, very aged storyteller in the next village not far from here. She knows all the ancient tales. I am sure she will have whatever answers you seek. My son will fetch her for you. It will take only two cups of tea.'

Wijaya considered this for a while. And then, perhaps because of the words the old man had chosen, about finding answers, he gave a single nod. 'Bring us the tea, then.'

The wizardly man with the daylight in his hand had been right so far, about meeting a messenger.

Wijaya and Mira were escorted to the biggest hut, where they were given seats, and had cups of some sort of green tea placed in their hands.

'Divine!' said Raden, relishing his drink. 'You'll enjoy this, young djinn.'

Mira tasted the tea. It was disgusting, smelling like cow. She decided to just hold the cup in her hands and pour the drink on the floor when no one was watching.

***

By the time the prince had finished his second cup of tea, a young man of about Mira's age appeared at the door of the hut. With him was a very old woman, her face a nest of lines.

'Here is the storyteller. Her name is Madam Sondakh,' he said.

The old woman moved to sit opposite them.

Mira was pleased to see that Raden Wijaya, despite his great rank, showed some deference to the poor old woman. It comforted her that he had a streak of politeness in him, which was probably rare in the olden days, when royal people often seemed to have chop-off-their-heads attitudes, or so it seemed.

Wijaya turned to Mira.

'So ask her,' he said. 'Ask her to tell me the story that I need to hear.'

The girl faced the old woman and bowed. 'Honourable storyteller madam,' she said. 'Can you tell us the story of the thief king of the Spiral River?'

The woman sat unmoving. No reaction.

Mira repeated the question. 'Can you tell us the story of the thief king of the Spiral River, please?'

This time the woman responded. 'No,' she said, simply.

Mira was frustrated. 'You don't know it? Are you sure? It would be really helpful. It's probably about some king in the olden days who—'

'I did not say I did not know it,' said the old woman. 'I said that I cannot narrate it to you.'

'Why can't you?'

In response to this, Madam Sondakh simply turned her head to look directly at the prince. She said nothing.

There was silence for a moment, and then Raden Wijaya broke it. 'You don't tell stories of the old kings, in case the current generation of royal family members is upset or insulted by them—is that the case? There are secret laws preventing you sharing such stories, is that correct?'

The woman's wrinkled face twisted slightly, in what Mira realised was the equivalent of a smile.

'I have lived many years,' she said in her low, slightly raspy voice. 'My preference is to live a few more, if I may.'

Wijaya leaned forward. 'As a member of the royal court, I hereby give you full permission to tell your stories of past royalty, without fear of punishment, or any negative repercussion. You have my word, in front of these witnesses.'

'Even if they are unflattering? Very unflattering?'

'Particularly if they are very unflattering,' said Wijaya. 'For then they are more likely to be the truth.'

The old woman tilted her head and narrowed her eyes slightly, intrigued by his attitude.

He continued, 'Good rulers are those who realise that people who criticise them are the people they can best learn from.'

Mira nodded enthusiastically. She was liking this guy more and more. Here was a cool guy who would make a great king. He definitely had a bit of nobility about him, trickster or not.

'Then I will tell you the story you wish to hear,' said the old woman. But before beginning, she turned to look at the villagers, several of whom were in the hut. She barked a few commands in what was probably the local dialect, and sent everyone else out of the hut.

When she was alone with Mira and Raden Wijaya, she began her story.

4

The Thief-King of the Spiral River

Nothing on earth, it is said, can make a mother give up a child.

A mother will undergo any hardship, forgo any pleasure, sacrifice everything she owns, give up her fondest dreams, and even her own life, to ensure the health and happiness of her child.

However, there is one and only one reason for which a mother can be persuaded to give up her baby. And that is, if she comes to believe that giving it up is the only way to save it.

Solomon, said to be the wisest king who ever ruled, knew this. And he used this principle to solve a puzzle over two women who claimed the same baby. 'Cut the baby in half,' he declared. One woman approved. The other said that she would rather give up the child than see it hurt. She had passed the test of motherhood—and Solomon had solved a mystery.

There was another mother who struggled with a similar question and came to the same dark answer: that her baby could only be saved if she gave it up.

The young woman, let us call her Nata, was the mother of a child who seemed to her to be special in some way. He was like a container, waiting to be filled with light or dark. His fast-moving eyes were as deep as oceans.

Nata felt that if he came to be filled with light, he would be a second sun, shining over the land. And if he was filled with darkness ... well, it was important that such a thing should not be.

The young woman saw that she had been given an extraordinary mission by destiny—to raise this miracle child, and she saw that she was destined to fail it.

For Nata was a peasant of the poorest sort. She was married to a Brahmin Gajapura, but they were humble people.

That summer, the rains failed. A blight had attacked their few surviving crops and they were left with no hope for themselves—or for the child of light and darkness that had been left in their hands.

What to do?

Once the baby had been weaned off his mother's milk, they needed solid food for him.

But there was none.

For days, the young mother was left with an impossible choice. There was barely enough food for one person, but she had to split it between two. Which two?

She had to feed the baby, there was no question about that. She had to feed her husband, or there would be no food at all for tomorrow. But if she starved to death, who would take care of the baby?

The answer came from the world of stories. She heard tales of babies in baskets, floating down the river—and being adopted by kings or queens, empresses or pharaohs.

No mother would want to take such a risk with her baby, but there were two factors that made Nata consider this idea seriously.

First, there was the baby's striking looks—he was a beautiful child. Anyone who looked into his face could see that this was a special baby, an infant who would change the world. Even when she took the child around the village, she could see the way people's eyes were drawn to him.

Second, there were the child's shrinking limbs and distressed eyes. He was not getting enough food and she came to realise that it was her duty to sacrifice her own role as mother to someone else to let the boy prosper.

And so, the next morning, she headed out to the Spiral River.

This great waterway, known as the River of Brantas on the maps, was a torrent of mountain water with a curious flow.

It started from its mountain sources flowing southwest, but then turned south, and then southwest, and then north, and then east. It formed a broken circle, shrinking in diameter—a spiral shape.

Anything placed into the river would flow a long way—but would end up not far from where it started. If she placed it in the Spiral River, perhaps she would see her child again, if the Gods should be so kind.

Nata and her husband lived near the poorest stretch of the river. There was nothing in their vicinity but poor fishermen, rocky riverbanks, and an old cemetery. But downstream, they knew, there were many fine towns and many wealthy people.

'This child is destined for greatness, we both know that,' Nata said to her husband. 'We must leave him in the hands of Heaven and trust that he will find his home.'

And so the child was wrapped in a blanket, placed in a basket-boat, and sent out onto the water with many tears and prayers.

And off he floated.

But destiny had its plans for the baby.

The basket-boat came ashore, not in a wealthy landowner's riverside garden—but in the cemetery on the outskirts of the town.

It was a place where no one went by choice, as it was said

to be haunted. And there was movement in the cemetery that night—but it was not a ghost, although the way the figure moved, lightly and almost invisibly, slipping through the shadows, it seemed like one.

A man of the shadows picked up the basket and saw the baby inside it.

Nata had been right about one thing—whoever looked into the baby's eyes would want to adopt it.

And so, the child was adopted by Lembong, a thief who lived in a small hut in the cemetery, among the graves and ghosts. He was a man as dark as the night in which he moved.

Lembong loved the child and shared his food with him—but more importantly, gave the boy the only thing of value he had: his skills as a thief.

The child, called Kenn Arok, grew quickly and picked up his adoptive father's talents speedily.

By the time he was nine, he could slip into any house, locate the best-hidden valuables in minutes, and spirit them away with no trace that he had ever been there.

And soon, he could outdo his father. By the time he was thirteen, Kenn Arok had become the king of thieves.

And as he came into full adulthood, the young man had built himself a reputation in the town near the cemetery, which was called Kediri, as a clever and dangerous man who got anything he wanted, one way or another.

Kenn Arok caused so much heartache and loss that his name began to be spoken with fear.

The local judges, unable to catch him, sent for help to the capital. The rulers of the land sent agents to capture him, but none could do so.

Kenn Arok would simply vanish from sight, slipping away and disappearing.

And so the situation continued for years.

But it turned out that while cunning could not capture the king of thieves, kindness could.

One surprising morning, Kenn Arok met a holy man, Mpu Lohgawe. The priest saw the light in the thief's eyes and realised that there was something powerful, almost god-like there. He appealed to the young man to listen to what he had to say.

The holy man, known as a rishi, taught Arok about good and evil, about right and wrong, and about the supreme importance of choices.

'The choices you make will connect you to something far greater than yourself,' the man said. 'The good road is the hard road—the narrow road—but it is the right road, and ultimately, it is the only road.'

Kenn Arok heard the message. It struck deep within

him touching the light that still glimmered, unseen, in a heart filled with darkness.

He spent time with the rishi and, slowly, the light within him grew.

One day, under a sky which was deep blue and cloudless, the king of thieves gave up his sinful ways and pledged to start life anew as a servant of society.

The holy man was delighted. He arranged for his convert to work as an attendant to one of the powerful feudal lords of the area, Tunggul Ametung, squire of one of the great cities nearby.

Kenn Arok became a good worker, married a local woman, and settled down to a new life.

The king of thieves was no longer a creature of darkness with a spark of light inside of him. He was now a creature of light.

But there was still a spark of darkness within him: a black flame, a reverse candle, a dark flicker shining in the hidden depths.

That shadow stayed out of sight—until one windy day when he was walking through the gardens of Tunggul Ametung's palace, and came upon the bathing pools.

There, he saw the most beautiful woman he had ever seen. She had the face of an angel, and when the breeze blew against her dress, showing her long, fine legs, he was enraptured.

That day was cloudy, but sunlight shone on the young woman.

Kenn Arok, when he had time off from work, went to his teacher, Mpu Lohgamwe, and asked him to tell him what the sight meant.

The rishi knew immediately whom he had seen.

'You have seen Kenn Dedes, the most beautiful of Tunggul Ametung's wives,' he said. 'And the light from heaven that shone on her is no surprise to me. She is a child of destiny. It is her presence that will make her husband a great king. Tunggul Ametung is but an ordinary man, but her wife is marked by fate for greatness.'

Kenn Arok bowed and took his leave.

The dark flame quickly grew in his soul until it became a fire.

He made a decision: he would win Kenn Dedes. He would be the person whose power would be enhanced by her beauty. He would take over the position of his employer as local ruler.

But first he had to make his biggest theft of all: he had to steal a princess—a squire's wife!

Kenn Arok needed a plan. As the king of thieves, he soon knew exactly what he had to do.

He contacted the greatest swordmaker In the land and asked him to make a kris for him—a ceremonial dagger. 'It must be the most beautiful kris in the world,' Kenn Arok said. 'The most ornate and the most eye-catching.'

The swordmaker started his task, gathering the finest metals, smelting them, and working on the most complex design he had ever attempted.

The work took several weeks, and Kenn Arok began to feel impatient.

And then he heard that Kenn Dedes was pregnant. This made him feel even more anxious to possess her as soon as possible. When she began a family, it must be *his* family. He would be the ruler, she would be his consort, and the child would be their prince. Now he had a deadline.

He went to see the swordmaker.

'Is it ready? Surely it must be done now!' he asked. 'You have taken weeks to make a single weapon!'

The swordmaker nodded. 'A weapon is not simply a tool,' he said. 'It carries with it the power of life and death over humanity.'

'Yes, yes, but is it ready?'

'Physically it is finished. But a weapon is not an ordinary object and should never be treated as one. It is an instrument of destiny. For this reason, I need to perform some rituals.

They will ensure that the kris is used only for good, and never for evil.'

The black flame inside Kenn Arok roared silently.

'I need it now.'

The swordmaker refused. 'You see this as the least important part of the process, but in truth, giving a weapon its destiny is the most important part by far. Its destiny is dark until the prayers that turn it to light are uttered.'

The king of thieves asked to see the weapon. He held the beautiful blade in his hands.

And then he spun on his feet and used it to stab the swordmaker in the heart.

The man fell to the ground.

As the life bled out of him, he looked his murderer in the eye. 'By your actions you curse the sword, and you curse yourself. The sword you wield will kill you,' the swordmaker said.

The king of thieves left the factory and quickly travelled home.

Back at the palace, Kenn Arok raced to the house of a rich courtier, who he knew collected weapons.

'I have a gift for you—the most beautiful kris in the world,' he said.

The courtier was thrilled with it. He turned it over and

over in his hands. And then the man ran off to show it to his friends and family, as the king of thieves knew he would.

Two days later, Kenn Arok was practising his once-dormant skills once again.

He slipped into the courtier's house and stole the decorated silver kris that he had given him.

Then he broke into the bedchamber of his lord and master, Tunggul Ametung.

'Hello,' he said to the sleeping man. 'And goodbye.'

He stabbed him in the heart and held the knife in place until the man died.

Kenn Arok left the decorated blade in his master's body, and slipped invisibly out of the room.

He stayed by the side of the building, in the shadows, waiting for the scream of the servants who would eventually discover the body of their ruler.

It came at dawn.

The king of thieves made sure that he arrived on the scene at the same time as the others who had heard the cry.

And he made sure he stayed silent until other people in the palace had identified the murder weapon.

'That dagger—I know who it belongs to!' said one.

'The chief courtier,' said another. 'He showed it to me yesterday.'

Kenn Arok made sure he was nearest the door, so that he reached the courtier's house before anyone else.

When the others arrived, they found Kenn Arok stepping out of the room, wiping blood from his hands. 'He confessed to the murder,' he said. 'I was so angry I killed him on the spot.'

He appointed himself head of the investigation into the killing while everyone was still in shock.

Kenn Arok pretended to ponder the facts of the case for a day and a night—and then found the courtier to be the killer, and he himself, of course, to be the hero: the man who had brought vengeance down on the murderer. He comforted the dead man's wife.

And, dear listeners, you can guess the end of the story.

The holy man had been right.

Kenn Dedes did become a queen, and her glorious light did shine on her new husband.

Kenn Arok rose to power and eventually become overlord of the whole land. The king of thieves had become the thief king.

But there is another ending to this tale, tucked into history, not many years down the line.

For the child that Kenn Dedes bore, of course, was not really the child of Kenn Arok at all.

The son also carried a bright light within his soul, albeit

a smaller light: the light of his lovely mother. He found that it contrasted with the shining darkness that his adoptive father carried.

The boy found the kris that had been used to kill his real father.

This young man went quietly from place to place, asking questions. He was told about the dead swordmaker and, slowly, he unravelled the truth.

And then he bided his time. The youngster waited for the right moment to kill his stepfather ... with the kris that the swordmaker had fashioned.

And so the dying artisan's curse came true.

As the full story came out, people were shocked, but of course they were glad that the thief king was gone. They dared to believe that the darkness that Kenn Arok carried within him would now be gone from the kingdom.

But they were wrong.

So great had his power been that a certain quality of darkness stayed in the palace, manifesting itself among the young generations as mischievousness, and among the adults as lethal cunning.

The elders saw this, and hid the tale of the thief king, forbidding anyone to share the tale ever again, upon pain of death.

And the story disappeared.

5

The Sea-eye

Marko Lee walked briskly up the hill—at first. But after five minutes' steady uphill climb, his legs began to feel heavy and he dropped his pace.

He was a nerdy, bookish boy, and tended to avoid sports if he could help it. Yet he had repeatedly found that when he was forced to do some physical exercise, he found he actually enjoyed it. Isn't that the way things so often go?

A game of football was horrible to contemplate, especially when you are one of the smallest, puniest boys in the class—but once it was actually under way, it could be good fun, and his size was often an advantage when it came to tackling other players. He could whiz through small gaps between his other taller classmates, and then dive under the flailing limbs of the opposition to take the ball from their feet.

Still, marching up a steep hill would probably never be fun, no matter how you looked at it. He realised that the sea was just over the ridge, so at least he might get a nice view—

and even better, he'd get a cooling breeze. It was *so* hot here.

For a moment, he had a vision of a little stall at the top selling ice cream and chilled drinks, as one often finds in tourist spots.

But then he remembered that they had gone back in time. Had stalls for tourists even been invented in the year 12-whatever-it-was? On what date did it say in his book had the Majapahit empire been founded? Was it 1293? Or sometime close to that?

Was it stupid to expect a drink at the top? Perhaps not. There must have been tourists for as long as there had been civilization, and that means thousands of years. And there had been commerce for thousands of years too, so maybe there would be some sort of tourism service at the top of the hill.

Though surely not serving ice cream and chilled drinks. What did they have in the olden days for tourists? he wondered. Maybe water or fruit juice or one of those historical drinks you read about, like 'mead', he thought. Whatever! Any kind of drink would do. And if there was nothing, he would just enjoy the breeze until he got himself rested and cool again. And then he would march down the hill to find his sister. There must be some fruit trees in the forest that would provide some sort of refreshment. He'd find a blackberry bush. Those were not that difficult to find.

As so often happens with hill walks, what seemed to be the top of the ridge actually led to a slightly higher ridge, and that one led to yet another peak.

But eventually, after another twelve minutes of steady climbing, Marko reached the top of the hill.

There was no drinks stand of any kind there, but Marko didn't notice. His attention was taken by what he did see: a stone tower, two to three storeys high, and an extraordinary view of the ocean.

The sea was vast, as seen from here—indeed, it was such a wide view that one could just about detect the curvature of the earth on the horizon.

Marko approached the tower and found a little stone staircase leading up to its upper floors. It was so quiet that he couldn't imagine there was anyone else around.

So he was surprised when he climbed the stairs and his head emerged into a stone room—and he saw a woman there, peering out of the window. The youngish woman, draped in a variety of mismatched clothing, was mumbling to herself, and seemed to be in a rather agitated state.

'Excuse me!' said Marko.

The woman didn't react.

'Excuse me,' he said, a little louder.

She turned, showing him an excited face underneath a mop of shaggy hair. 'Ship approaching. Go tell General Irawan,' she barked. 'Right now! And if you can't find him, tell Pakubuwana.'

'Oh. Right,' said Marko. 'But can I have some rest first? I came straight up this hill, from the bottom, and just need a minute to catch my breath.'

The woman's eyes widened. Clearly this was not the response she expected.

'I just told you. You need to go and tell ... wait ...'

She turned back to the sea and stared at it, her right hand shading her eyes.

'No. I've changed my mind. Come with me.'

She marched to where he stood, and he moved backwards as quickly as he could, down the steps, even skipping a few in between.

Then the two of them were standing outside the look-out tower.

She grabbed some sort of leather garment from a box nearby and threw it around her shoulders.

'Come on,' she said and headed across the top of the hill.

'Where are we going?' Marko asked.

There was no response and the boy wondered why the woman had not shown any surprise on seeing him.

Marko realised that it was probably not unusual for a boy to suddenly turn up at a look-out post. In this era, boys of his age were probably low-ranked functionaries of some sort, who ran between various people to do errands, deliver messages and so on. She probably thought he was a member of the same army or defence force that she was part of.

She led him to a different route down the hill, the side facing the water, and he scrambled to follow her. She had clearly made the journey often, finding confident footing down a steep and irregular path cut through the bushes.

Marko was less confident on this track, but his small size and lightness on his feet meant that he could spring from rock to rock and descend in her wake, without letting much distance grow between them.

'Where are we going?' he asked again, his eyes on his fast-moving feet.

No answer.

They eventually marched out onto a flat, pebbly beach and he saw that they were moving towards a boat that was moored on the shore.

'Go to the other side,' she barked.

The two of them pushed the boat into the water, and then jumped in. 'My shoes and socks are soaked,' he complained. 'The salt will be bad for the leather.' But by that time, he was feeling so hot that the cool sea water was pleasurable rather than unpleasant.

He realised that the woman was so intent on doing whatever it was that she needed to do that she barely noticed he was there. He was just a tool, like an oar or a rudder. You don't explain to an oar or a rudder where you are going, or what your plans are for the day.

After they were about fifty metres away from shore, she gave him both oars and told him to row them steadily forward. She then turned to stare ahead.

Marko had the horrific thought that she expected him to row the boat right across an entire ocean—there were no landmasses in sight, so there was nothing between them and the horizon. They seemed to be heading directly out into the open sea.

'Where are we going? To the horizon? You can't really go to the horizon as such,' he said. 'The horizon retreats from you. So, the more you go towards it, the further it goes away from you. It kind of remains at a set distance. It's basic physics.'

But she was not listening.

'It's because the world is round,' he continued. 'Actually it's a globe. But I don't know whether science has discovered this yet in this day and age. Is it 1293? Or somewhere around then? Although I know that the Greeks were aware of it—some of them, anyway. I mean the fact that the world is round. I could explain how it all works to you, if you are interested. But maybe not.'

She was staring so hard into the open sea that he realised she was not listening. He might as well have just been part of the breeze.

He continued to row. His arms were aching by now, but he imagined the workout must be good for him. Maybe he'd get muscles, and look like a superhero.

In the tower she had mentioned something about seeing a ship. They must be going to meet the ship, he thought. He hoped that they were not going to confront the ship. One boy and one woman would have no chance against some sort of enemy navy.

Then she spoke.

'The Sea-eye has been wrong once and only once, boy,' she said. 'So I am not going to be wrong again.'

'Is that your title? The "Sea-eye"? I guess you are like a professional look-out person, right?'

Again there was silence, except for the rhythmic splashing of the oars, and the now-distant roar of the waves on the sandy beach far behind them.

She spoke a little later. 'After a great storm a year ago, I saw something on the horizon that I didn't recognise. And I knew all the local fishing boats were in harbour. So I sounded the alarm.'

More silence.

Marko waited patiently for the rest of the story.

But now she was shading her eyes again and looking at the horizon.

He narrowed his eyes and tried to follow her gaze. But he could see nothing. The horizon was a simple flat line.

'I sounded the alarm,' she eventually continued. 'But it turned out to be a great tree that had been ripped out of the ground by the storm and sent into the water. I couldn't understand how it could even float, it was so big and so heavy. But it did.'

'That was the only time you were ever wrong? Well, that's a pretty good score,' Marko said in an encouraging tone. 'One wrong out of however many right?'

The Sea-eye shook her head, dismayed by the memory. 'It was the only time I was ever wrong,' she said again, distantly.

Marko had a thought. 'Was there a big storm recently? More trees falling into the water? Is that what we are going to check?'

She turned to look at him.

'Are you telling me you didn't notice the rain two days ago?'

'Ah,' said Marko. 'There was a storm two days ago? Ah, well, you know, I sleep really heavily. I often sleep through things, even thunder and lightning. My sister says ...'

He saw she had stopped listening so he drifted into silence. She leaned forward out of the boat, as if even a tiny bit closer would help her identify whatever it was she saw on the horizon.

'The Sea-eye has only been wrong once,' she repeated. 'And I am not going to be wrong again. This time I am going to confirm that it is an enemy ship before sounding the alarm.'

Enemy ship!

'Where is it?' asked Marko, anxious to take a break from rowing, which was now making his arms hurt really bad. Was something dangerous ahead of them?

She pointed to the horizon, slightly to the left of centre. 'See that dot on the horizon?'

He stopped rowing and just stared at the distance for a while, glad to have his glasses on, and happy to give his arms some rest.

'I can't see anything that way,' he said. 'But I can see a dot over there.' He turned his body and pointed to the right.

She turned her head and followed his finger.

And then she spoke in a breathless whisper. 'Another

one. Two enemy ships. But why are they so wide apart? Why are they not together in a convoy?'

Marko narrowed his eyes and shaded them with one hand, scanning the whole horizon.

It occurred to him that his vision, with the aid of glasses, might be as good, or even better than the vision of an adult woman who lived in a period before spectacles had been invented. He would make a good Sea-eye himself. He wondered how much a Sea-eye got paid.

'There,' he said, now pointing to the left. 'Another one. There are *three* ships, all spread out.'

She wrinkled her brow. 'I don't understand why are they are not together. In a convoy. For safety.'

And then her face changed. Her eyes widened. Her jaw dropped open.

'Back to shore! Now! *Now!*' she screeched.

He tried to turn the boat around, just pushing with one oar, the other hanging out of the water. It was not easy.

He felt her push him out of the way as she grabbed the oars and took over the job herself.

She was soon rowing as fast as she could.

Marko found a second, smaller pair of oars in the back of the boat, and helped row with those. There was an air of panic in their little boat, and it made it easy for him to disregard the ache in his arms.

'The Horde!' the Sea-eye mumbled to herself. 'The Horde is coming. It can be no other.'

'That's not good,' said Marko, just to be saying something. He was feeling nervous now.

After a few more minutes of steady rowing, they were picked up by the waves and delivered on the beach. He turned to look behind him.

The entire horizon was lined with dots—there were scores, maybe hundreds of ships. The open sea was filled with danger, heading straight for the bay where he and his sister had been taken.

'Who are they?' Marko asked.

'The Mongol Horde are known as the most dangerous killers on the earth,' she said. 'They leave no one alive.'

'Oh, bother!' he said, as they jumped out of the boat onto the sand and started running up the beach.

6

The Coming of the Horde

Marko burst through the door. 'Thank goodness we found you—we have to hide!'

The woman behind him spoke with scarcely less excitement. 'The Horde is coming. They are less than an hour from shore.'

The people in the room leapt to their feet, except for the old storyteller, who merely angled her head to look at the newcomers with curiosity.

Raden Wijaya noticed that Marko addressed his words initially to the young woman who was seated next to him. And then he realised that they had similarities—he had features similar to her, and was wearing equally odd clothing of a strange material.

'A djinn assistant of yours?' he asked.

'My brother,' said Mira. 'I mean, yes. My brother, as in my fellow djinn or angel or whatever. All djinns are brothers and sisters. That's how it works.'

The woman known as the Sea-eye scanned the room.

'My lord, where are your men?'

'They're around,' said Wijaya, rather languidly. 'I sent them back to the main encampment to get some rest while I came here to gather some information. I have had a measure of success, thanks to this messenger. Although I still seek a map.'

He didn't seem to be worried about the fact that they were alone and unguarded, and a very large number of enemy troops was approaching.

'Where is the Horde?'

'Maybe close to the beach by now,' said Marko, breathlessly. 'There were hundreds of ships, and probably thousands of fighters. Maybe tens of thousands. We'd better run for it.'

'The boy's right,' said the Sea-eye. 'There is a very large number of landing craft. There are several hundred ships, stretching the full width of the horizon. I have never seen such a big fleet.'

They stepped out of the small hut where they had been listening to Madam Sondakh and walked—way too slowly and calmly in Marko's opinion—in the direction of the fields. Several of Wijaya's men had been posted in the village and he called one of them over.

'Go to the encampment. Get General Pakubuwana and the captains. Bring them here. No, tell them to get on the main road to the beach. We're heading there now. We'll all meet at the edge of the clearing and then meet the Horde together.'

The Sea-eye spoke with urgency. 'My lord, you cannot meet them with just your commanders. You need the full troop; as many men as you can muster. These people do not know how to negotiate. They are famous for destruction, for slaughter. And you know why they are here.'

Wijaya nodded. 'I know why they are here.'

But he refused to be hurried or panicked. And he continued to walk at a slow but steady pace towards the water.

A long way behind, Mira fell in step with her brother and they updated each other on what they had discovered.

'This is Raden Wijaya,' Mira said. 'He is like a relative of the ruling family. But the family is deposed and a new king has taken over. A guy called Jayakatwang killed the ruling family. I think Raden is not very happy about it,' she said. 'There's a huge battle going on right now, but then he heard from a holy man that he needs to come here and meet me. Guess who the ...'

'Ha!' said a voice behind them.

It was a soldier, a young man of about seventeen, who was walking close behind them. He had overheard Mira's speech to her brother.

'Not very happy about it,' he mocked. 'That is one way you could put it.'

The two children turned to look at him.

'We don't really know what's going on,' Marko said. 'Can you fill us in? Give us a bit of history?'

'Yes, please,' said Mira. 'I have this homework assignment that you wouldn't believe.'

The thin teenager looked rather odd in his ill-fitting fighter's leather jerkin, which was clearly designed for a larger, older man.

He introduced himself as Keruas.

'First, can you tell us what year it is?' Mira asked.

'I'm guessing 1293,' Marko said.

'School tutors these days are hopeless,' the young man muttered. 'Teach you nothing. Not like in my day. Yes, the year is 1293, if you go by the spice traders' way of counting, although we use a different system here.'

Mira was stung by his critical attitude.

'Actually, I know a fair bit more than you might think,' she shot back. 'I know that Raden Wijaya's other troops are trying to take over Tumapel, but he came here to learn the story of his great-grandfather. Most people don't know the story because it's, like, censored, but I know it. I'm one of the few. And I also know that Raden Wijaya is here to found a new kingdom called Majapahit—'

The boy held up his hand. 'Majapahit?'

'This kingdom. Isn't that what it's called?'

The boy looked puzzled. He shook his head. 'No such place,' he said. 'You are confused. Majapahit is a type of fruit. This kingdom is called Singhasari.'

Mira looked dismayed. 'Now I'm confused again.'

Marko leaned towards her and whispered, 'I think we may be in right at the beginning of the Majapahit Empire. It hasn't been founded yet. It was founded and given its name this year.'

He held on to her arm and pulled at her.

'You're slowing me down,' she complained.

'I know,' he said. 'I don't think we should be going towards the beach.'

'Why not?'

'The Mongol Horde. Do you know who they are?'

'I've heard of them. Is it like Genghis Khan?'

The young soldier behind them was still eavesdropping. 'Yes, but Genghis Khan is dead. His son, Kublai Khan, is now the leader.'

A thought struck Miranda Lee. 'The guy in the poem? Didn't we have to study a poem about him a few years ago?'

Her brother nodded. 'Yes, only in the poem they spelt his name a bit differently. How did it go?'

Mira recited:

In Xanadu did Kubla Khan
A stately pleasure-dome decree:
Where Alph, the sacred river, ran
Through caverns measureless to man
Down to a sunless sea.

She gave her audience of one a smug smile, pleased with herself to have remembered the lines.

'I liked the opening bit, but the rest of it was a little baffling,' she added.

Her brother spoke with irritation.

'Anyway, the poem is not the main thing. Getting away from this lot is the main thing.' He dropped his voice to a whisper. 'The Mongol Horde troops can be really nasty.'

Mira slowed down. 'Maybe you're right. They don't sound very nice. I mean, if you are a group of nice people, you wouldn't describe yourself as a horde, would you? The word has negative implications, right?'

'You know how a zillion different movies all start the same way?' asked Marko. 'There's a peaceful village and the bad guys ride in and they kill everyone and burn all the buildings?'

His sister nodded. 'Yes, and the guy or girl who is going to be the main character in the movie is just a kid at the time and he is watching from a distance and he pledges to take revenge on behalf of his parents, etc. Yeah, lots of films start like that.'

'Well, that part of the story is based on the history of the Mongol Horde. They were the main people famous for doing that. That's what they do. They swoop into villages and kill people and burn houses.'

'Kinda violent.'

'Not kinda violent. SUPER violent. I'm telling you, we do not want to be anywhere near them.'

She frowned.

'But if they are super dangerous, why is the prince just walking towards them with only a handful of soldiers?'

'I don't know, but I think we are all going to die very soon. We should get away.'

The two children tried again to surreptitiously break away from the group walking towards the waterfront.

But then, Keruas, who was still just a few steps

behind, pulled out a short, curved blade and pointed it directly at them.

'You don't want to do that,' he said. 'Getting lost on the way to the battle is not a good idea.'

'But listen! It might be dangerous,' Marko said. 'There are hundreds of them. We wouldn't want children to be hurt, would we?'

'Fighting for your kingdom is dangerous, with death as a possibility,' said Keruas. 'Desertion is even more dangerous. The punishment is death, and that's a certainty.'

The children kept walking.

7

A Devious Deal is Made

What would they do? Mira realised that if they could not get away, their only chance would be to warn Raden Wijaya that the horde was a highly dangerous enemy. They didn't have history books here or TV documentaries, so he probably had no idea.

After all, he hadn't even known about Kenn Arok, who had been king of the place just a few generations ago. There was clearly no freedom of information here.

'I think we need *way* more troops on our side,' Mira said to Keruas. 'There's no way so few of us can battle hundreds of ships worth of Kublai Khan's killer soldiers. We need to turn back, find more people to join our side. These guys are *mean*.'

'Keep marching,' Keruas said. 'If Lord Raden Wijaya wishes us to meet them on the beach, that's what we will do. I think it is better if you speak no more.' He raised his knife again.

'I'm shutting up,' Mira said quickly. 'I'm zipping it, see?'

She made a zipping gesture with her fingers moving across her lips.

'I don't think they have zips here,' Marko said. 'They seem to have various fastening methods, such as—'

'Stop talking!' Keruas barked.

Silence descended for a while.

'How far to the sea from here?' whispered Mira.

'About ten minutes,' said Marko.

'Then I reckon we have ten more minutes to live.'

***

Two hours later, they sat with the troops at a campfire on the beach.

The confrontation they had expected between Kublai Khan's men and the Raden Wijaya's troops had never happened.

The Mongol ships, it turned out, had three generals, and one of them had come to meet Wijaya. They had greeted each other as old friends.

Mira had realised that Raden Wijaya had clearly inherited some of the "trickster" genes of the thief king of the Spiral River.

Here he was, in a secret friendship with a group of people who were reputed to be the darkest enemies of his kingdom.

Later, as darkness fell and the army cooks set up cooking

stages and campfires, Keruas told them that the troops had now been briefed on the whole story.

'Most of us were kept out of the loop. Lord Wijaya is good at keeping secrets,' he said.

Raden Wijaya was definitely a trickster prince, with a smidgin of the spirit of Kenn Arok in him.

'So what have you learned?' Mira asked.

'The master has somehow recruited the Horde to come and help fight against the king. The Horde has been hiding in bays nearby for some months, recovering and restocking after their long journey—and of course preparing for the battle. Raden intended to send one of his generals, Pakubuwana or Irawan, to meet them and escort them to the main city—but then he decided to come himself.'

'Our grandfather told him to do that,' Mira said.

Marko was fascinated. 'But I don't get it. The Mongol Horde are famous—they over-ran much of the inhabited world. Didn't they create the biggest empire in history or something? Why would an army so powerful and so violent want to come and help some guy down here in South-east Asia overthrow his leader? What's in it for those guys?'

Keruas laughed.

'Lord Wijaya is a tricky one,' he said. 'He has a plan. He always has a plan. A year ago he asked his adviser, a man named Arya Wiraraja, regent of Madura, for help and advice. Wiraraja wrote a very enticing message to the leader of the Horde, the Great Khan. It said that the most beautiful princesses in the world live in South-east Asia. He said that the area was famed throughout the world for the beauty of its women—which is true. But he added that there were two princesses in particular who were so beautiful, known as the daughters of Tumapel, that it is said that at least one man a week dies from happiness just by looking at them.'

Mira was surprised. 'That can't be true.'

'It is true,' said Keruas. 'I caught a glimpse of them a few times. You can feel your heart beating faster or suddenly stopping. Their beauty can kill you.'

The girl's brow wrinkled.

'Doesn't sound like a good thing to me. I mean, everybody wants to be nice-looking, right? But you don't want to actually kill the boys who are just looking at you. I mean you'll probably want to marry one of them sometime. Possibly. And what about legal liability? If you are so beautiful that you kill people who look at you, couldn't a good lawyer demand compensation for his clients, the parents of the dead boys, and all that sort of thing?'

'When your beauty takes on mythical proportions, it is a good thing,' said Keruas. 'Anyway, Wiraraja wrote to Kublai

Khan promising introductions to the most beautiful women in the world—if he sent three groups of soldiers to help him take over the kingdom. Kublai Khan clearly decided this was a good deal.'

'So all these troops are just coming because Kublai Khan wants a new girlfriend?'

Keruas thought about this for a moment. 'Actually, there is another reason, and one which might be even more important. The Great Khan has not liked the ruling party of this land for some time. A little over a year ago, Kublai Khan sent a ship down here with a senior official from the court. The official wanted to know if the land would become a protected vassal state of the Khan, and pay tribute, in return for protection. The leader of this region replied harshly. He branded the official.'

'What do you mean branded? Like a designer label thing?'

'No! Branding—placing a mark with red hot metal.'

'Ouch!'

'He made a mark on the official's forehead and then sent him back, saying, "This is my reply". Of course, the Khan was very angry. So he needed to take revenge against the ruler of this place.'

'So that's another reason why the Horde is here?'

'Sort of. In fact, the ruler who branded his official was

Kertenegara. But Kertenegara is dead. The current king ...'

'Jayakatwang!' interrupted Mira.

'Yes, Jayakatwang, formerly leader of the vassal state of Kediri, took his place. But he is as heavy-handed and unpopular as his predecessor—which is why most of us, meaning *us, citizens*, want Lord Raden Wijaya to take over the kingdom. Rulers need to be more than strong. Bullies are strong, but bullies do not make good leaders. A leader needs to have nobility, leadership, wisdom—and kindness. He has to have a moral heart. Otherwise, the ruling administration eventually turns as foul as its leader.'

Keruas was surprisingly philosophical for a young man. And he knew his history, too. The children soon discovered that the teenager was the son of a temple priest, and had been educated for years before joining the army as part of the rebellion.

Mira borrowed an exercise book and a pen from Marko's school bag and took notes.

Some 20,000 to 30,000 men from Fujian, Jiangxi and Hugang in North Asia were gathered by Kublai Khan the previous year, and set sail, landing on the coast of Java the previous November. (It takes months to sail from Mongolia to South-east Asia.)

There were about 1,000 ships, and they were originally

stocked with provisions for a year. Three of the main groups in the region were represented, each with a leading officer: the Mongol leader was Shi-Bi; the Uyghur leader was Ike Mese; and the Chinese leader was Gaoxing.

By the end of the year, all the ships had decamped from their original landing spot and set up base in other secret coves away from the main coastal cities.

One ship had been destroyed by hitting rocks, but the men had swum to safety to one of the islands. Fortunately, among the pieces of cargo that had survived the wreck was a box of tools. So some of the men had cut down trees and made another boat for themselves and rejoined the main army. Others had stayed on the island and married local women.

By the beginning of this year, they were swapping secret letters with Raden Wijaya and plans were afoot for the invasion.

And now, in March of 1293, the fighting had begun. Wijaya and his cohorts had been battling in the main city for sometime.

Lord Wijaya had assigned his deputies to lead the fighting, and then he himself had headed to the coast, after having received advice from a holy man that this was what he had to do. As they had approached the water, he had seen a majapahit tree standing on its own.

This was appropriate because the area of land that he had been designated as his was in the region called Trik (or Tarik, or Tirik, depending on your dialect). But the part that had been carved out for the central encampment was in a forest of majapahit fruit trees.

So when he reached the coast, north of the capital, and saw a majapahit tree, he knew that was where he should wait for the messenger—and be ready to greet the Horde.

And, just like the wise old man had predicted, he had been greeted by a djinn called Mira who had led him to learn the secrets of his ancestry.

After that, right on cue, the Horde had arrived: his secret partners who would ensure that he would win the war.

Now it was time for them to travel back to the capital city—and join the final battle.

8

The Look-Out Post

Wars are not good places for children. Battles and youngsters are both inherently unpredictable. And the human psyche is such that even the most hardened army commanders would be discomforted if their side included youngsters who needed to be protected.

Raden Wijaya had appointed Mira and Marko Lee to a non-combat division known as scouts. This group in turn was divided into three sub-units—one of which explored the edges of the main battlegrounds; another formed a retreat guard, making sure that the troops were never approached from behind; and the third took what was known as "high ground look-out duty".

Mira and Marko were in this third group, and their job was to find the highest points of the city so that they could get a view of what was happening—and then send messengers with useful intelligence to the battle leaders at the front.

Thankfully, because of the way the city was on one side

of a hill, the look-out scouts were a fair distance from the actual skirmishes, so there was not too much violence in their field of view. Mira was grateful for this. She knew that her little brother fainted at the sight of a drop of blood, so he would not do well in an actual battle.

Keruas was appointed head of the high ground look-out sub-unit. Although it had been several years since he turned fourteen—the official age of adulthood for men in that society—Raden Wijaya obviously still thought of Keruas as a youngster and wanted to keep him safe.

The battle raged for a full day, and Mira and Marko watched most of it from a hilltop—or to be more accurate, from a tree on top of the hilltop. As the lightest, nimblest people in the look-out group, the two children had been sent up the nearest tree so that they could get a better view of the fighting in the valley below.

As dusk fell, it became hard to see—but the arrival of the Horde had definitely turned the battle in the favour of the usurpers.

Not only were the Horde fighters terrifying in themselves, but they also had an extraordinary weapon—some kind of fire-stick.

They held some sort of metal tube in their hands and they would do something at one end. The result would be a loud bang and a projectile would fly at high speed out of the other end. The projectiles did enormous damage to the enemy.

'They have some sort of hand cannons or fire-sticks,' said Keruas. 'We have never seen such things before. But I have heard people talk about them.'

'We call them guns,' said Marko. 'I read about this in a book. The first guns were invented in East Asia right about now. This might be the first, or one of the first wars ever, in which guns were used. Pretty amazing if you think about it.'

Keruas shook his head in amazement.

'The fire-sticks can throw death,' he said. 'They can throw death right across a field. At a very fast speed.'

Jayakatwang's men had spears, but they were slow and relatively inaccurate. They would fly into the air and move in an arc-shape. The Horde fighters could see the spears coming, and dodge them.

But the hand cannons were different. They shot death out in what seemed to be almost a straight line, at high speed.

And any soldier hit by one of the projectiles would be flung backwards—even if he was wearing armour.

'The fire-sticks are powerful magic,' said Keruas.

The only part of the battle which was causing concern to the usurpers was the area around the palace. While the

Mongol Horde had attacked furiously and taken over much of the city within hours, there were still some hold-outs in and around the main complex of the rulers.

'We're going to attack the palace,' Keruas said. 'It's a smart move. If we catch their leader, the last of the king's soldiers will be demoralised. They may switch sides—I've seen that happen before. They start to realise that their only chance of survival is to be on the winning side, so they turn around and start fighting for the other side.'

'But I guess the king will be well-guarded,' said Marko.

Keruas nodded. 'Yes, and the palace is large and connected to several other buildings. It'll be hard to find the king.'

'Look,' Mira said. 'Is that Raden? He's going into the palace's main entrance.'

The prince, distinctive in his brown-purple cloak, ran through a field filled with some sort of burning material, probably oil, and into the palace gate.

The watchers held their breath for several minutes—and then they saw a blur of purple again. He was racing out of the palace, but he had something on his back—something wrapped in brightly coloured silks.

Keruas laughed out loud. 'He's stolen a princess,' he

said. 'The glorious daughter of Tumapel is his—one of them, anyway.'

Mira clapped her hands. 'His great-grandfather stole a princess too,' she said. 'Only he did it in a really nasty way, not like our guy.'

'Do you mean Kenn Arok?' Marko asked.

'Yes. Did you read about him in your book?'

The boy nodded.

'He was actually Raden Wijaya's great-great grandfather,' Marko said. 'Let me try to remember ... yes, two or three greats, I think. And I think he may have been related through marriage, rather than directly, but either way, I don't think there's any DNA there. I think Wijaya was Kertenegara's son-in-law, so he kind of married into the family.'

'Who cares about those details, or how many greats there are?' his sister asked.

'You do,' he replied. 'Or you should. If you get it wrong, you'll lose marks in your essay.'

Miranda didn't reply. She did not want to be reminded of her homework. 'We're in the middle of a war, for goodness' sake! Typical of nerdy you to talk about homework.'

The girl screwed up her eyes and squinted at the scene. She realised that the prince was running through the flames with a princess on his back. He really did seem to be fearless.

They saw him race across a field, jump over a small stone wall and then into a clump of trees—at remarkable speed, considering he was carrying a person.

'Is he going to take her to safety now?' asked Mira, who now had a bit of a crush on the prince, although she admitted that he was an elderly man by her standards.

'I don't know,' said Keruas. 'There are two princesses, you see—they are sisters. He's probably trying to make a decision. Should he go back in and try to find the other, or should he take the first one away from the battlefield?'

Marko leaned forward.

'Are the sisters the ones who are so beautiful that you die if you look at them?'

Keruas nodded. 'They're all like that in the royal girls' room,' he said, and then added with a hint of laughter in his voice: 'Or at least they think they are!'

In the last bit of fading light, they saw a small group of people heading due west from the trees, and another group heading back to the palace.

The instructions to the high ground sub-unit were to re-join the other units when night fell and it became impossible to see anything in the darkness.

'We need to go now and re-join the others,' said Keruas. 'It's useless to stay here in the dark. The sun has disappeared.'

'No, wait,' said Marko. 'There's going to be a full moon tonight. We'll still be able to see.'

'Are you sure?'

Mira nodded. 'Yes. This is a full moon period. Trust us, we know about the full moon. We're kind of fans.'

Keruas agreed to wait. And sure enough, in less than 20 minutes, the clouds had parted to show a ghostly grey moon shining down on the city.

After their eyes had adjusted to the different light, they got back to work, with each of them looking down on a different group of streets.

They watched for another few minutes in silence. Then Marko gave a shout. 'Look! There.'

Keruas and Mira followed the line of his finger to see a shadowy group of people coming out of the east wing of the palace's main building.

'I bet that's the king or some general or somebody important trying to escape from the palace.'

The furtive group was heading directly towards what looked like an outer wall of the complex.

'I bet there's a secret door there,' said Mira. 'They don't know you can get out of the palace grounds that way. That's why none of our lot's troops are covering that area.'

Keruas leapt to his feet. 'We need to go and tell them. We're probably the only people who know.'

He asked Mira to stay with the other members of the group until they returned. He took Marko with him and said he would teach him a special technique that messenger-runners used.

'You decide on a route as a pair, to start with,' the teenager said. He pointed to a path down a hill which ran between two crumbling buildings and then veered to the right.

'We'll go down there, follow the path to the right, and then when we come to that fork, we'll take the left one. That should lead us to our soldiers' encampment behind those trees, and to where Lord Wijaya is.'

The messengers' running technique was simple, he said. 'Your body can move quickly for a short while or it can run slowly and steadily for a longer time,' Keruas said.

Marko nodded. 'Where I come from, we call that sprinting and jogging respectively.'

'This is what we do: we set off together. One of us runs the first half at high speed and the second half at a slower speed. The other runs the first half at a slow speed and the rest at a faster speed.'

Marko thought about this. 'But what's the point?' he asked. 'It doesn't get the message to the right person any faster, does it?'

'That's right,' said Keruas. 'But the advantage is that the runners are never together. So if one gets taken down by enemy soldiers, the other has a chance of getting through. About half the scout-runners in a battle get killed.'

Marko gulped. 'Oh. Right. Ok.'

They set off running down the hill. Then Keruas sped up and disappeared into the distance. Marko jogged along at medium speed, saving his energy for a sprint later on.

Best not to think about this too much.

He kept jogging steadily for several minutes and then eventually reached the turn in the road they had identified as the half-way point.

Then he speeded up, running for his life.

He could hear screams and shouts as the fighting continued all around him.

And then, from time to time, there would be a loud crashing sound as the world's first handguns were fired.

This was not fun.

Marko narrowed his eyes so that he could see less of the scary scenes around him and started running, quite literally, for his life.

9

The Princesses of Tumapel

Two weeks later, the weary party arrived at the township in the forest of Trik.

After winning the battle against King Jayakatwang, many people expected Raden Wijaya to install himself immediately in the palace as the new ruler.

But that didn't happen.

Wijaya had gone into the palace and spoken to the troops from a high balcony of a tower, where they would all be able to see him.

He had explained that this was to be the start of a new era, where things would be done carefully and thoughtfully, with the needs of the whole community uppermost in the minds of the governing elders.

'Jayakatwang divided his time between the dining room and the palace ladies' quarters, as did my relative Kertenegara before him,' he said. 'That is not the right way to govern a great land and a great community of people.'

He said that he would go through a crowning ceremony to become the new king in two weeks' time.

The period would give a breathing space for a number of important jobs to be done.

Leaders would be invited to travel to Tumapel from all over the land, so that they would become part of the new governing process.

High priests would be drafted in from around the country, so that the unseen world would also play an important part in the ceremony.

An advisory committee would be set up so that the leader would have the wisest men to help him make the decisions that needed to be made.

And the Horde would have to be paid for their part in helping them win the war.

After the speech, Raden Wijaya had set his lieutenants to work in the palace and the nearby government headquarters, while he took the majority of the surviving army members aside so that their wounds could be tended and they could spend a few days in recovery.

After a week of this, they set off to return to his former headquarters, the new town of Majapahit in the forest of Trik.

It was on this journey that Marko realised that something was wrong.

Everyone had become very tense. There was much

whispering and people stood in separate clusters during the evening encampments.

The feeling of triumph after the victory had vanished like snow falling into a hot spring.

'The party spirit didn't last very long,' said Mira, looking at the grim-faced men putting up their tents for the night.

Something had gone wrong.

Marko didn't reply at first. He nodded slowly. He was a sensitive boy and was very conscious of the change in demeanor in the group of people.

After surviving his job as a runner in the battle, he thought nothing would ever worry him again. But the haunted look in the eyes of the soldiers was making him uncomfortable.

'People are really worried about something,' he said. 'I think we should go and find out what the problem is.'

They quietly wove their way in a figure-of-eight pattern around the soldiers' tents until they found Keruas.

He was busy in a meeting with a group of other young soldiers, so they waited patiently until he was finished. 'You want to talk to me?' he asked, leading them away from where the men were talking, and towards a campfire.

'What's the problem?' Mira asked. 'Everyone's so gloomy. People look like someone just died.'

'Lots of people did just die,' Marko said to her. 'These guys were just in a war, remember?'

Mira put her hand to her mouth. 'Yeah, right. I guess that was kind of a stupid thing to say. It's just something we say in—where we come from.'

Keruas poked the fire at which they sat with a stick before responding.

'No one is happy. You see, the Mongol Horde has given Raden Wijaya a list of their demands for helping us overthrow the king. And they are ... difficult to meet.'

'Oh,' said Marko. 'That's bad news.' He looked into the fire.

'They should have agreed on terms before the battle,' said his sister. 'I would have done. That's the *proper* way to make an agreement.'

'Wait,' said Marko. 'Didn't they agree to introduce the princesses of Tumapel to Kublai Khan or something? Wasn't that the deal?'

Keruas stirred the fire again, his face heavy.

'That was part of the deal,' he said. 'Raden promised friendship and co-operation between the two kingdoms in the future, plus an introduction to the princesses. But they want a bit more than that.'

They waited for him to continue.

He looked over at the generals' tent, where Raden Wijaya was talking to Pakubuwana before speaking again.

'They say that acceptance of their services is confirmation

that our kingdom is now a vassal state of the Great Khan.'

'That doesn't sound good.'

'And we have to pay tribute for protection every year—a sum to be paid in gold and goods and ... people.'

'Ouch.'

'And they want *all* the women of the royal court to take back with them now. They want them to be given as gifts to Kublai Khan.'

Mira stood up.

'That's outrageous! You can't treat women as property! You olden days' guys really don't get it. I hear this kind of thing all the time and it's wrong, wrong, wrong!'

Keruas was taken aback by her sudden outburst.

She wagged her finger at him. 'We would in no way stand for that where we come from. What about women's rights? What about girl power? I hope you are going to refuse and tell them where to stick their offer,' she said.

The young soldier looked puzzled. 'Where?'

'That's something else we say where we come from. It means ... er ... that you don't like something. We don't literally mean bottoms.'

Keruas' face took on the same puzzled expression that Mira saw so often when talking to people on their journeys.

'Put it this way,' the young soldier said, poking the fire again. 'The terms are impossible to agree with, and even if

Lord Wijaya did agree to them, he has developed a personal relationship with one of the princesses of Tumapel, as a second wife—and there is absolutely no chance of him giving her up to the Mongol Horde.'

'He's probably more scared of her than he is of them,' said Mira.

Keruas' eyebrows rose.

'Never mind,' Mira continued. 'That's probably way too modern a joke for your era.'

'That one I *do* get,' Keruas said, 'but I wouldn't make it myself. We need to respect our leaders. But yes, the princesses are strong-willed and powerful people. A wise man would never cross one of them.'

'So what are they going to do?' asked Marko. 'I mean about the Horde's demands?'

'We have a problem,' the young man said. 'The only possible response is to fight them.'

'Yep. Send them packing,' said Mira. 'That's yet another modern expression that you won't get. I seem to be full of them today.'

'Never mind my sister. She's crazy,' said her brother. The boy's brows had knitted together and he was staring into the fire again. 'Okay, now I see why everybody is so gloomy.'

'Because they don't want to start fighting another battle, so soon after the previous?' his sister asked.

'No,' said Marko. 'Because no one has ever beaten the Mongol Horde. You fight them, you lose. If Raden Wijaya is saying that we should fight them, then we will lose.'

The soldier nodded.

'Correct,' he said. 'The Horde is impossible to defeat. Especially now, with their fire-sticks. You cannot stop them. And once they win the fight, they usually slaughter everyone. Sometimes they kill all the males and take the women away as prizes for themselves, which is what they will probably plan to do on this occasion.'

Miranda Lee sat down. 'Not looking good,' she said. 'Not looking good. We really ought to be thinking about getting home. Only we need to see Lord Wijaya at least one last time, so we can deliver something to him.'

***

In the end, the children were interested to hear that Raden Wijaya called upon the spirit of his great-great-grandfather, the thief king of the Spiral River, as their only hope.

Everyone knew they would not be able to win a war against the Horde, a practiced army with ferocious strength and an unbeaten record.

So their only chance of success would be to use cunning. They would have to trick their enemies in some way.

After a day of plotting, they put their plan into action.

The two princesses of Tumapel and the other ladies of the court were installed in a building in a new town being built in the forest of Trik.

A message was sent to the Horde saying that the royal ladies were exhausted by the battle and by the journey to the forest. The visiting army should thus come and escort them to the boats, in which they would be transported back to Kublai Khan.

In order to not traumatise the women any more, they had decreed that there should be no weapons anywhere in the area. The women had seen too much blood and they did not like it. There would be no weapons in the building, and the Horde representatives who came to get them should be carrying no weapons.

The unarmed representatives should arrive at noon the following day and the signed documents and two women, the Princess Tribhuwana, known as Parameswari, and Princess Dyah Gayatri, known as Rajapatni, would be presented to them.

'Why does everyone have so many names?' Mira complained. 'How am I going to get all this right in my assignment?'

'It's a royal thing,' Keruas said. 'You just have to learn them.'

***

In event, the plan worked only partially. The Horde sent representatives to fetch the documents and women—but the full army stayed very close behind.

And when Raden Wijaya's men attacked, it became instantly clear that the Horde had concealed weapons everywhere.

They were instantly back at war, but this time Raden Wijaya's exhausted troops were fighting against an unbeatable army armed with high-tech weapons.

Fighting raged the whole day and most of the night, with the groups dividing into two separate areas. The Horde held the area close to the water, where they could get regular supplies from their ships. Lord Wijaya's men formed a protective shield around the princess of Tumapel and their retinue in the inland forests.

There was a lull in the fighting the second day, but the third day the Horde seemed to find new strength and managed to pick off many of Raden Wijaya's best troops with fire-sticks.

Mira and Marko, being too young to fight, stayed with the princesses, but received regular reports from the front lines, usually from Keruas or one of the other young men.

Raden had ordered the messengers to tell the truth to the princesses about the progress of the fighting, but much of the news was bad.

Early on the morning of the fifth day of fighting, the news was particularly depressing.

'We're barely managing to keep them at bay,' said Keruas, addressing his remarks to Princess Tribhuwana, who was the leader of the royal retinue. 'They are exhausted from all the fighting, as we are. But the Horde fighters do seem to be unbeatable, especially with their hand cannons. Every day our numbers go down by a lot—and their numbers hardly fall at all. If this continues as it is, we will eventually lose. It is inevitable.'

The fighting continued for another day.

At dawn the following morning, the messenger reappeared, exhausted and limping.

This time Keruas's news was worse—the battle was about to be lost. 'Lord Wijaya says that all members of the royal retinue need to be ready in case the order comes to flee into the forest. If that happens, messengers will accompany you to safety.'

Then Keruas bowed low.

'But it will be other messengers, not me. Today it is my turn to join the front line. So I take this opportunity to say goodbye, as I may not return. It has been my honour to serve you.'

The older princess, Tribhuwana, bowed her head, and the younger one, Rajapatni, curtseyed. Everyone looked stricken. Keruas had become popular with the royal party.

'Can't you stay and guard us?' the young princess Rajapatni asked.

He shook his head. 'It is my turn to fight. Even if I could change that, I would not.'

Then he turned and marched out of the grounds.

Mira and Marko went out of the house to watch him disappear onto the forest path that led to the beach, where the main fighting was taking place.

'I hope he makes it,' Mira said.

'Me too,' said her brother. 'He's a good guy.'

But that morning, the sky was thick with clouds as if the darkness of the night did not want to give way to a new day.

And then it started raining heavily.

'Bad sign,' said Mira. 'When it rains in the movies, you know something really bad or really sad is happening.'

Marko gave her a look of irritation. 'This isn't the movies,' he said. 'It might not mean that at all.'

There was an ominous crash of thunder and the rain started falling heavily.

Or maybe it did: that was the message that nature seemed to send. The two children went back indoors.

***

Late that afternoon, Keruas and two of his colleagues were

back, ragged and wounded but alive—and were thrilled to be bringing surprisingly good news.

'We couldn't defeat them,' he said. 'But the storm could. The Horde is getting back into the ships to leave.'

Mira's eyes widened. 'What? They were scared of a bit of rain? I haven't been scared of thunder and lightning since I was a child. Pathetic.'

'You *are* a child,' Marko said, elbowing her.

'*You're* a child. I'm a young woman. There's a huge difference.'

She looked up at Keruas. 'Wait. You're really saying that the storm made them give up and run away?'

'In a way,' said the young man, shaking his head so that the spray of rain shot out in all directions. 'Sorry. I didn't mean to get you wet.' He was addressing his apology to the princesses.

He then wiped his head on a piece of cloth, that a lady-in-waiting handed him, before continuing.

'The storm is the marker for the start of the rainy season sea-change. The currents change course. The monsoon winds blow from the south at this time, but not for long. The doldrums move and the sea-lanes have to adapt. All sailors know about this.'

The younger princess smiled at him. 'But how does that affect the fighting of the battle?'

Keruas turned and pointed to the trees visible through the open door behind him. 'See how the trees grow at an angle, slightly bent to one side, but the wind is now blowing them the other way? The sea-change is beginning. It will be in full force within six weeks. The Mongol Horde leaders realised that if they did not head back north now, they would be trapped in South-east Asia for another six months. They do not have enough food to last that long—and with us, as a hostile force on land, they were concerned that this would be the last chance for them to head back to their home country with at least some of their cohorts intact. They too have lost many men, perhaps two or three thousand by now.'

The listeners digested the news with delight on their faces.

'They have very good shamans on board, who can read the weather,' Keruas continued. 'All agreed that this was the monsoon change. They must return now or be trapped by nature.'

'That is a stroke of good fortune,' said the young princess.

Keruas bowed. 'Our fighters could not defeat them. But with the elements on our side, they could not stand against us.'

Later that night, Raden Wijaya returned to the young township in triumph and celebrations took place for hours.

At one point, late in the evening, Marko strolled up the leader at the banqueting table, and said, 'Excuse me, Lord Wijaya. As a student of history, let me congratulate you on your achievement. You might be one of the few people in history to defeat the Horde.'

'I had help,' said the new king. 'The gods were on our side.'

Mira joined them. 'We've got something for you,' she said. 'I've been trying to give it to you for ages. A little present from the old guy you met in the temple—the one with blue light shining from something in his hand?'

Wijaya raised himself up. 'Your grandfather? What is it?'

Mira held out what looked like a large coin. 'He wanted us to give you this.'

Marko was suddenly alarmed. 'How did you get it out? I hope you didn't break the piggy bank?'

She shook her head. In her other hand she showed him the piggy bank, still in one piece. 'Nope. Not damaged at all. I took one of the banqueting knives and stuck it in the slot and managed to kind of wriggle the thing out.'

Raden Wijaya stared at the coin and traced the complex pattern of lines on one side of it.

'We're not sure what language it is,' said Marko. 'Can you work it out?'

'It's not a language at all,' said Wijaya. 'On one side is a sun symbol. And the other, I think, is a map of the palace. Anyone who has lived there would recognise it. It seems to be marking something, or showing the way to something. There's a certain symbol in one of the rooms behind the main hall on the carving. I'm hoping it will lead me to solving a few of the other mysteries of my ancestors. Please thank your grandfather for me. He is a remarkable man—perhaps the finest rishi in the land.'

His expression changed as he had a thought. 'Do you think your grandfather would be interested in working for me? I could give him an important role.'

Mira shook her head. 'He's always on the road. Never stays in one place more than a few days. He will already have gone.'

'That's a pity,' the new king said.

The children bowed once, and then started to walk away—but they were brought to a halt by a sharp word from Lord Raden.

'Wait. What is that thing you are holding?'

Mira turned and stepped back to him, showing him the piggy bank.

'Where we come from, we use these things to save money in.'

The new king took it from her and turned it over in his hands. 'A wondrous design,' he said. 'A boar of some sort. A most marvellous invention. May I keep it?'

Mira looked at Marko, remembering that earlier he had been very protective about the piggy bank.

Her brother thought for a moment and then nodded. 'I think it's fine. I think grandfather would be happy for you to have it.'

His sister suddenly grabbed his arm.

'Look,' she said.

The boy followed Mira's upward gaze and saw what she saw. The storm clouds had parted and moonlight was shining down on the party.

'It's time to go,' Marko said.

They took their leave of Lord Wijaya, who would soon be crowned as the new ruler of one of the biggest kingdoms in history, and walked away to a quiet spot where they wouldn't be seen.

'Can I just see if I can find Keruas?' Mira asked. 'I want to say goodbye to him. After all, I won't ever see him again.'

Marko shook his head. 'He's talking to the young princess, I'll bet. But anyway, the gap in the clouds is really small,' he said. 'We don't have much time.'

She looked up and saw that her brother was right. She gave a deep sigh and glanced over to the tent where Keruas was talking to Rajapatni.

Mira was sad to leave. She hadn't found herself a prince, but she had found a cool guy to spend time with, not much older than she was. And they'd had a huge adventure together. In a way, she and Keruas had fought together in a war. That was something worth remembering. She'd always have that.

'I guess you're right,' she said to Marko. 'Let's go.'

He pulled the magic mirror out of the bag and gave it to her. She held it up to the sky. The moonlight filtered through the strange metallic plate and bathed the two children in its growing magical glow.

10

A Valuable History Lesson

Two days later, Mira and Marko were walking through the school gates when they saw the new history teacher, Mr Tork, ahead of them.

The girl was so excited, she ran up to him.

'Mr Tork, did you read my history essay yet? Doing it was really fun.'

He turned and raised one eyebrow.

'I think this is the first time ever that one of my students has described a major homework assignment as "really fun",' he said. 'But I'm glad to hear it. I haven't read the essays yet, but I am looking forward to it.'

He had crinkles around his eyes and an odd moustache that curled around the edges of his mouth. But his expression was friendly and he smiled as he walked with them through the school grounds.

'What historical event did you chose in the end?' he asked. 'Did you find an unusual one?'

'Yes, a really good one. Did you know that most of South-east Asia, including Indonesia, Malaysia, Singapore, Brunei, East Timor, and bits of Thailand and the Philippines, were all once part of a single kingdom named after a fruit?'

He looked surprised.

'That's news to me! I know that at various times there have been empires spanning a few of these places, but a fruit? Are you sure?'

She grinned. 'Yes. The massive Majapahit empire, which started in 1293, takes its name from a kind of fruit. "Maja" is the name of a kind of fruit and "pahit" means bitter, so "bitter fruit".'

He nodded. 'Ah, I see. The Majapahit empire—a challenging choice. I didn't know that was where the name came from. But I know there is some exciting history in that tale. Why did you choose that?'

Marko interrupted. 'Boys,' he said with a laugh, 'there are so many handsome princes in that story. She likes handsome princes.'

Mira turned and glared at her brother. 'Rubbish. That had nothing to do with it.' She looked back up at Mr Tork. 'Actually, our grandfather kind of suggested it. He thought it might be interesting, and he was right.'

The teacher said, 'It's certainly a fascinating period of history. But there's not much information available on it. It's something that people really should know more about. How did you do your research?'

This was always a tricky question. Mira and Marko had only told very few people about the magic mirror and their journeys. To everyone else, they just kept that part of their research out of their accounts of how they educated themselves.

'Well, you get bits of the story from different documents,' she said. 'There are the historical sources, which tell us that Prince Raden Wijaya took control of the area from a nasty ruler called Jayakatwang in 1293.'

She tilted her head as if remembering something. 'Raden Wijaya was a seriously cool guy. Usually I don't like old guys with thick black moustaches, but he was kind of okay. Nice eyes and all that. As they say.'

The teacher's expression showed surprise at the comment, but he said nothing, and the girl continued.

'Raden Wijaya was the one who really expanded the kingdom using the name of a fruit tree in the forest of Trik. Before it became Majapahit, it was called Singhasari. But there are the fairy tale stories too. It's all part of the history of the place.'

Mr Tork looked at her. 'What do you mean by that?'

'There are old collections of stories, such as the tale of the thief king, Kenn Arok, who was an earlier ruler, and the tale of the Kleting sisters, which comes a bit later, under the rule of someone else. Some of these you can tell are fiction, but others seem to be, er ... de ... de ... what's the word ...?'

'Derived?'

'Yes, derived from real historical events. And they were written relatively close to the actual events they covered. So Kenn Arok would have been a real ruler, even though the details of his life are tucked into tales which read like stories.'

The teacher smiled as they reached the steps to the main building.

'Very good. People often make the mistake of dividing things into fact and fiction, when, in reality, in historical writings, they overlap a great deal, and there are things we can learn from all types of sources. I believe there are some Chinese sources too—about the Mongol invasion of Java in 1293, seen from the North Asian view.'

'Yes!' she said. 'That was *so* exciting. There were three fleets that arrived—a Chinese one, a Mongolian one and a Uyghur one. They set off in the year 1292 and then arrived in Java, and hid in the bays until they were ready to attack. And they helped Raden Wijaya defeat Jayakatwang—but then they ended up battling each other.'

This time both the eyebrows of the teacher went up.

'My, you *have* done a lot of research,' he said. 'And what's your opinion on why they decided to help this man who lived far south of their own country?'

'There were a few reasons,' she said. 'One of the earlier kings of Java had insulted their envoy, or so I was told. There was also a bit of romance involved, with the Great Khan being told that he would be introduced to the fabled princesses of Tumapel, said to be the most beautiful women in the world.'

'The most beautiful women in the world? That sounds like a worthwhile asset to collect,' laughed the teacher.

'I didn't think they were that beautiful. I would give them maybe eight out of ten on the cuteness scale.'

'Rajapatni was prettier,' said Marko.

'Rubbish,' his sister said. 'She had an annoying voice. Princess Parameswari: *she* was the beautiful one. And she had a nice voice.'

'No, Rajapatni any day.'

The teacher looked baffled at this.

'You've seen a movie or something?'

'No.'

Before she could answer further, there was an interruption.

'Oh my goodness!' said her brother.

'What?' said Mira, suddenly annoyed at the way he was interrupting the conversation.

'Look at this,' said Marko, handing her the tablet computer he was holding. 'I just looked up something on the internet and found this.'

Mira took the computer and Mr Tork looked down to see what was on the screen.

It was a report about a piggy bank, centuries old, that archaeologists had found in Indonesia. Although the style of the artefact was surprisingly modern, this particular example had clearly existed hundreds of years ago, and had been dated to the period of the kingdom of Majapahit, the article said.

'How odd,' said Mr Tork. 'They had piggy banks there! Who would have thought?'

'We'll have to buy a new one,' Marko said.

Mira glared at her brother. He really needed to shut up.

'Well, I look forward to reading your essay,' Mr Tork said. 'I know it's going to be a good read. What was the most interesting thing you found out about Majapahit?'

The girl thought for a moment.

'The rulers were nice to women,' she said. 'In the olden days, people were often not very nice to women. But they were a bit cooler in Majapahit. In one of the books I read, it said that some of the descendants of Raden Wijaya who became rulers were female. So that's cool.'

'Definitely a good thing,' said the teacher.

'Also, there was a lot of evil in the empire. The ruler Kenn Arok was a trickster, and there was much hatred for him for years. But I think that changed with Raden Wijaya. He was still a bit of a trickster, but with him it was not deceit, but cunning and cleverness. He had a good heart. At least that's how I see it.'

'And nice eyes,' said the teacher.

'Yeah, so true.'

Marko put up his hand.

'I helped her with the research. What I found interesting is that there are many signs of Majapahit culture still visible, although people don't realise it. Like the portal gates of Bali, and stuff like that.'

The teacher was impressed.

'I think I may ask the two of you to give a presentation to the school about this. I think we can all learn from it. Good work, you guys.'

As the teacher took his leave, disappearing into the school hall, Mira turned to her brother.

'Funny about the piggy bank,' she said. 'I wonder if we

delivered it from now to the past, or whether it came from the past and we just took it back.'

The boy nodded slowly. 'That's a puzzle. I'll have to think about that one.'

She turned away from him to head to her school locker, but he called her back.

'Mira,' he said. 'I need to show you something.'

He took the magic mirror out of his bag. 'Look at the edge.'

Every time they went on a journey, they found a new word on the edge of the metal disk. This time the word was *Go*.

'I wonder what it means.'

'You know what it means,' she said with irritation. 'Or have you stopped speaking English?'

'You know what I mean,' he said.

'Class is about to start. I have to go.'

'Me too.'

Marko's first class was science. He decided he would ask the physics teacher about time travel and stuff. The whole issue about the piggy bank intrigued him.

The sun shone through the window on the small, excited boy, as he walked briskly to the science lab.

A Note from the Authors

Don't read this first! There are spoilers in it. So read the book first, and then turn to this page.

Done reading the book? Great. We really hope you enjoyed reading *Magic Mirror: The Prince of Tricks*. We loved writing it.

One of the great things about this series is that all our stories are based on real things that happened.

And it is often the case that the things that are hardest to believe are the things that are most firmly rooted in history!

We did invent Miranda and Marko Lee, but they are also real, in a way—since they represent anyone who is interested in learning about history: we hope that's you!

And magic mirrors, with their curious properties, are definitely real. You can find pictures of them on the internet, or look in museums for actual examples.

As for the story of the kingdom of trickster princes, almost all the historical details in the tale are straight from ancient records.

Ancient books tell us about Kenn Arok, the thief king of the Spiral River, and you can look at the shape of the Brantas river, which still flows today, and is still the same shape. There are different ways of spelling his name, so if you want to find out more, some sources list him as 'Ken Angrok'.

Raden Wijaya was also a real prince, and he really did win the throne from the ruler, Jayakatwang, and steal away the beautiful princesses of Tumapel, although again there are various versions of the event, and no one knows exactly which one is most accurate.

The part about the Horde arriving in ships and hiding on the coast, before joining Raden Wijaya in his fight, is also taken straight from history.

And so is the story of the final battle, in which Raden Wijaya's men end up fighting the Horde, but only win the battle when the weather eventually causes the enemy to abandon the fight.

But perhaps the strangest thing of all is this: we think of piggy banks as modern things. Yet archaeologists found an ancient piggy bank among the artefacts of the ancient lost kingdom of Majapahit. It seemed oddly out of place, and no one knows its real history. We didn't make that bit up.

We love puzzles like that—they just go on to show what a fascinating world we live in!

We hope you enjoyed this tale enough to collect all the *Magic Mirror* books. And look out for the next in the series—see you next time!

Luther Tsai and Nury Vittachi

Hong Kong, 2016

"A small disk made of stone, a bit like a big, thick coin. It looked very old, and had the design of the sun on one side, and some odd lines on the other, like a pattern made of squares and rectangles."

The Surya Majapahit (The Sun of Majapahit) is thought to be the symbol of the Majapahit empire. It's found in many ruins dating from the Majapahit period. The eight-pointed sun ray with a circle in the centre symbolizes the cosmos - A beautiful circle of stone to represent the universe.

"On one side is a sun symbol. And the other, I think, is a map of the palace."

The palace of Raden Wijaya has never been found. But the pattern made of squares and rectangles is taken from real palaces. These were designed by American Architect Frank Lloyd Wright, and known as the "textile block houses" inspired by the Mayan civilization of South America. The thrill of time travelling with a Magic Mirror can be enhanced on the Internet as you search up the people and places Mira & Marko discover and discover them for yourself!

Instructions: 1) Cut out all four pieces of the model. 2) Cut out the pink centres of the circle and sun pieces and glue the shapes on top of the black areas on the remaining disks. 3) Bend the black triangular tabs and glue them to disk pieces to create your own "Sun of Majapahit."

OTHER BOOKS IN THE SERIES

The Visionary Voyage
A Magic Mirror Mystery
ISBN: 9788184777864

The Traveller's Tale
A Magic Mirror Mystery
ISBN: 9788184778250

The Tomb of Time
A Magic Mirror Mystery
ISBN: 9788184770070

The Wall of Willows
A Magic Mirror Mystery
ISBN: 9789351030072

The Shining Scripture
A Magic Mirror Mystery
ISBN: 9789351031352

The Chess Pavilion
A Magic Mirror Mystery
ISBN: 9789351037088